D0593490

A Woman's Walk in Truth

Vonette Bright

HARVEST HOUSE PUBLISHERS

EUGENE, OREGON

A WOMAN'S WALK IN TRUTH

Acknowledgments

I have such joy in the opportunity to reach you in your homes through the ministry of the "Women Today" radio program that airs on more than 500 stations. Thank you for listening!

There are many people who help me make this radio program possible. I want to especially thank Chris Shenk, the production manger, and Larry Hauer and Mary Mattingly, who lead our Communications team.

I owe a tremendous debt of gratitude to Evelyn Gibson and Jim Sanders for faithfully coaching me so we can provide a quality program.

This book would not exist without the folks at Harvest House Publishers. Bob Hawkins Jr., LaRae Weikert, and Barbara Gordon have been such a great encouragement to me.

My love to Brenda Josee, who has believed in me and inspired me in so many ways. She worked tirelessly to adapt the radio transcripts into these devotions that I hope will encourage and inspire you to live Christ every day. I can never thank her enough for her friendship and her dedication in assisting me in so many ways.

Introduction

Dear friends,

If ever you needed to believe in the absolute truth of our sovereign God, it is now. But you must base your beliefs on God's Word alone, not on man's ideas of what God's Word does or doesn't say. Subjective truth can lead you down a path of confusion. Objective truth is focused on God and His character and will allow you to live your life with confidence in the One who created you.

The brief vignettes in this little book are intended to refresh your spirit, challenge your thinking, and hopefully motivate you to take each "This I Believe" statement to heart and make it your own.

Every day brings changes in what we are told to believe with certainty. How can we be sure of anything? The character of people we trust can disintegrate in a 24-hour period. Medicines we thought were surefire guarantees to help us suddenly become dangerous and are pulled from the market, institutions that once seemed impervious to corruption are exposed for fraudulent practices, and even Christians—yes, those we believed to be God-honoring—become disgraced publicly.

At my stage in life it's easy to spend time reflecting on all the amazing works of God. The realization of human potential is overwhelming. However, at the same time, I say with confidence that we are facing a crisis of belief. We must recapture the faith of our forefathers and restore confidence in our God, who is all-knowing and most certainly all-wise. My dear husband, Bill Bright, taught so well the attributes of a triune God and how we should see Him as Creator, Savior, and Judge.

What do you believe? When you begin each day, you go into it with certain presuppositions…you meet a schedule…you fulfill obligations to show up at work on time. Why? Because you believe it is the right thing to do. You feed your body because you are hungry, and you believe eating will satisfy that hunger. You act on what you believe. If Christians lived what they profess to believe, our world would be changed quickly. What about you? Do you live your life believing what you see or seeing what you believe?

Confidence in your Creator and the character of the God in whom you believe gives you the ability to act and live with purpose. If you think seriously about the challenges and opportunities of each day, it all comes down to what you believe. Do you believe there is more to life than today? Do you believe there is a Supreme Being in control of this world?

The contents of this book came from transcripts of the "Women Today" radio programs. As I re-read them, I added some comments from my heart to yours for you to consider. Please ask the Holy Spirit to help you accept the truth of God's Word so you can state with full confidence…

"This I believe!"

Lovingly,
Vonette Bright

75 Candles

Have you taken an inventory of what's important in your life? Birthdays are a great time to reflect and look forward. Imagine you were blowing out 75 candles on your birthday cake. What would you want to have accomplished by then?

Before Bill and I were married, I never would have imagined the Lord would use my husband and me so dramatically. God guided us to start Campus Crusade for Christ, an organization that has become a worldwide ministry with more than half a million workers.

Our goal from the beginning was to put God first in our lives and do all we planned for *His* honor and glory.

So, dear one, let me ask: Have you let God be the center of your life goals? Are you willing to let Him use you? Ask God today to take over *every* area of what you do. He will do a marvelous work with your life too.

Whether we are here in this body or away from this
body, our goal is to please him (2 Corinthians 5:9)

This I Believe
You can never go wrong putting
God first in everything.

Always a Reason

Stonewall Jackson was abandoned as a penniless orphan at the age of three. He grew up and, when a young man, enrolled at West Point. This man who would become a great Civil War general developed the habit of constant prayer. He once said, "I have so fixed the habit of prayer in my mind that I never raise a glass of water to my lips without asking God's blessing, never seal a letter without putting a word of prayer under the seal, never take a letter from the post without a brief sending of my thoughts heavenward."

In 1 Thessalonians 1:2, Paul wrote, "We always thank God for all of you and pray for you constantly." I encourage you to keep praying too. The everyday events of life can crowd out the ever-present reality of God. A quick, simple prayer brings life into focus.

When you fully depend on God, it is possible to have a prayerful attitude at all times. And just as Stonewall Jackson learned, you always have a reason to pray.

Always be joyful. Never stop praying. Be thankful in all circumstances, for this is God's will for you who belong to Christ Jesus (1 Thessalonians 5:16-18).

This I Believe
Every breath I breathe is the
essence of a prayer.

Anybody Listening?

Have you ever prayed and thought no one was listening? Think of God listening in this way:

It's like a little boy who begs a man for a dollar. If the boy is a stranger, the man will likely walk away.

When the same boy asks his daddy, since his father knows it will be used for a good purpose, he will happily give his beloved son the money.

When you ask Jesus Christ into your heart, God becomes your heavenly Father. He has promised that He will hear and answer the prayers of His children—including yours!

Have you asked God to be your Father? If you haven't, why not stop right now and invite Jesus into your heart? When you have, you can be assured He always hears you and will provide for your needs.

The LORD is far from the wicked, but he hears the prayers of the righteous (Proverbs 15:29).

This I Believe
My heavenly Father's love is ever present.

Attitude Is Everything

Attitude *is* contagious. Is yours worth catching? Bob and Kelly worked on the same sales team. Kelly was hopeful and optimistic. She viewed challenges as opportunities. Bob, on the other hand, complained about everything. If a challenge arose, he viewed it as yet another obstacle.

Bob noticed how Kelly responded during team meetings. She seemed to face everything with a calm peace. Finally he worked up the courage to talk to Kelly about her perspective. There, in her cubicle, Kelly explained that her attitude came from Christ. She shared her faith with Bob, and he prayed to invite Christ into his life!

Friend, your life speaks so much louder than words. And, fortunately, your attitude is something you can change quickly if you need to. Attitude is *everything*. Ask God to give you an attitude worth catching today.

> *Don't be selfish; don't try to impress others. Be humble, thinking of others as better than yourselves. Don't look out only for your own interests, but take an interest in others, too. You must have the same attitude that Christ Jesus had* (Philippians 2:3-5).

This I Believe
I can choose to reflect God's love every day.

The Best Prescription

Sharon was hospitalized with severe depression. She had even lost the will to live. One day she cried out to God in desperation. Then an unfamiliar woman came into Sharon's room. She took Sharon's face in her hands and said, "Jesus Christ can heal you."

Sharon never saw that woman again. But after she was released from the hospital, she started going to church and reading the Bible. She sought Christian counseling. Soon her heart was filled with joy and peace.

Psalm 42:1 says, "As the deer longs for streams of water, so I long for you, O God." As the life of a deer depends on water, so our lives depend on God. Oh, precious friend, whatever you're going through today, cry out to God in prayer. Fill your mind with Scripture and praise. This is the best prescription when you're feeling down.

*Why am I discouraged? Why is my heart so sad? I
will put my hope in God! I will praise him again—
my Savior and my God!* (Psalm 42:5-6).

This I Believe
My life and voice will praise the Lord today.

Betty's Bunch

As one of the youngest of nine children, Lisa was a shy person. But when she heard about a two-mile walk in Central Park to raise money for Parkinson's disease, she was interested. Her mother, Betty, had suffered with Parkinson's for the past 17 years. Lisa sensed God impressing her to show her mother support. She organized a group comprised of 53 family members and friends to walk in the fund-raiser. She named them "Betty's Bunch." And "Betty's Bunch" raised more than $50,000 and set two walk records!

At the supper before He was betrayed, Jesus basically told His disciples, "Friends, love is more than warm feelings. It's an attitude that reveals itself in action. Go the extra mile and share God's love with someone today." Who will you share Jesus with today?

> *[Jesus said,] "Now I am giving you a new commandment: Love each other. Just as I have loved you, you should love each other. Your love for one another will prove to the world that you are my disciples"* (John 13:34-35).

This I Believe
Today I will demonstrate God's love to someone.

Celebrating Freedom

Have you heard this saying: "A hero is no braver than an ordinary man—he's just brave five minutes longer"? How true that is! Our country was founded on many singular acts of countless ordinary people who believed in the value of freedom. They paid for the freedoms we enjoy and celebrate in the United States today.

And how true that saying is in our spiritual lives as well. Jesus Christ braved death on the cross. He paid the ultimate sacrifice so that we can be set free from the burden of sin. The Bible says, "If the Son sets you free, you are truly free" (John 8:36).

Freedom from sin brings many liberating benefits, including living without guilt and waking each day with hope. That's a truth certainly worth celebrating!

This is the day the LORD has made. We will rejoice and be glad in it (Psalm 118:24).

This I Believe
I will celebrate the joy of my salvation today by telling someone what Christ did for me.

Simple Prayers

As a mother and grandmother, I love children's prayers, and books with children's prayers in them. Here are a few of my favorites:

> "Dear God, please send me a pony. I've never asked for anything before. You can look it up!"

> "Dear God, we read in school that Thomas Edison made light. But in Sunday school they said You did it. So I bet he stole Your idea."

> "Dear God, the bad people laughed when Noah built a boat on dry land. But he was smart. He stuck with You. And that's what I'm gonna do too."

I love the simplicity of a child's heart for God. In fact, the Lord says we're to come to Him in faith, believing...as a little child. Do that, friend! Don't just *talk* about prayer; rather, spend time *daily* with the Lord and go to Him with the simple heart of a child.

> *[Jesus] said, "I tell you the truth, unless you turn from your sins and become like little children, you will never get into the Kingdom of Heaven. So anyone who becomes as humble as this little child is the greatest in the Kingdom of Heaven"* (Matthew 18:3-4).

This I Believe
With childlike innocence I trust God
to lead me through this day.

A Clean Slate

Nancy was walking in a park. She prayed God would lead her to someone who needed to hear about Jesus Christ. Soon Nancy met a young man named Jim. It turned out he had been a gang member and a drug user. He didn't think God would ever forgive him. Nancy shared how God had changed her life, and He wanted to do the same for Jim. Jim prayed with her and invited Jesus Christ into his life. That day God wiped clean the slate of Jim's sins. Jim became a new creation!

My friend, you may not think you are an evangelist, but God will give you the ability, courage, and power to tell others about Christ. Share the good news with somebody today. Help him or her discover the joy of being forgiven forever.

By God's grace and mighty power, I have been given the privilege of serving him by spreading this Good News (Ephesians 3:7).

This I Believe
God will use me in a special way today.

Encouraging People

How good are you at encouraging others? Author and scholar C.S. Lewis gathered around him aspiring young writers whom he instructed in the things of God's Word. One fellow's writings so amazed Lewis that he wanted to see them published. But the young author rejected the encouragement. He didn't think anyone would want to read his humble text.

Lewis took one of the man's stories to his own publisher anyway. They, in turn, were so impressed that they printed not only the story Lewis brought them, but any others the man was willing to write. What would have happened if C.S. Lewis hadn't encouraged this self-effacing author? Perhaps the world would never have heard of *J.R.R. Tolkien*.

I encourage you to take time to share words of encouragement with those around you. Tell them they are important to God!

Offer sacrifices in the right spirit, and trust the LORD. Many people say, "Who will show us better times?" Let your face smile on us, LORD. You have given me greater joy than those who have abundant harvests of grain and new wine (Psalm 4:5-7).

This I Believe
People need to be told how important they are to God.

Davina's Discovery

Davina lived in a spiritually dark neighborhood, so she began praying for her neighbors. It wasn't long before God's work became evident. One family stopped playing loud music. Some of her neighbors began going to church. And Davina shared Jesus Christ with another neighbor. But Davina didn't expect to see changes in her family. Her husband started leading family prayer times, and her daughter began telling classmates about Jesus Christ.

Davina's attitude toward prayer also changed. Now she is eager to spend quality time alone with God every day.

I hope you discover the power of prayer. Why not think of someone who doesn't know Jesus Christ, and then commit to pray for him or her every day? Ask God to work in his or her heart and life. And don't be surprised if He changes your heart too!

Confess your sins to each other and pray for each
other so that you may be healed. The earnest
prayer of a righteous person has great power and
produces wonderful results (James 5:16).

This I Believe
My heart is open to receive
what God has for me.

Delayed Obedience

Eric was a 16-year-old boy who liked to drive fast—despite his mother's stern warnings. One afternoon Eric was given a speeding ticket with a hefty fine. He began to drive slower, and even got a job to pay the fine. To his surprise, three months later Eric received a summons to appear in traffic court. He'd done all the right things. Unfortunately, he found out he'd waited too long to pay the money he owed.

Jesus *requires* your total and *prompt* obedience to what He asks. Delayed obedience is really *disobedience*. King Saul was told to wipe out the Amalekites and their animals. He didn't obey. When confronted, Saul alleged they'd saved the best animals to sacrifice to the Lord. But the Lord wasn't happy, and Saul lost his kingdom.

Friend, you demonstrate your love for God when you follow His commands.

> *Samuel replied, "What is more pleasing to the*
> *Lord: your burnt offerings and sacrifices or your*
> *obedience to his voice? Listen! Obedience is better than*
> *sacrifice, and submission is better than offering the*
> *fat of rams. Rebellion is as sinful as witchcraft, and*
> *stubbornness as bad as worshiping idols. So because*
> *you have rejected the command of the Lord, he*
> *has rejected you as king"* (1 Samuel 15:22-23).

This I Believe

My obedience will be an example to someone today.

Don't Keep It to Yourself

Every Saturday Susie goes to a nursing home and shares Christ with the residents. One week she met a 90-year-old woman named Margaret and shared the gospel. But Margaret wasn't interested. Susie prayed for her that week and during the next visit she said, "Margaret, if it were not for the Lord Jesus, I wouldn't be here. I want you to experience Him and spend eternity with Him too!"

That day Margaret finally said yes to Jesus. Only 11 days later she passed away and went to heaven to be with the Lord.

Dear friend, think of what heaven will be like. The Bible says there will be no death, pain, sorrow, or crying. Eternity with God will be more wonderful than we can imagine. So don't keep it to yourself. Take every opportunity to share Christ with someone today. You never know what tomorrow will bring. The only things you can take to heaven are the people you help lead to Christ.

He will wipe every tear from their eyes, and there will be no more death or sorrow or crying or pain. All these things are gone forever (Revelation 21:4).

This I Believe

I will carry the thought of heaven in my heart this day.

Excellent Woman

Rachel Saint's brother, Nate, was killed in the jungles of Ecuador. Savage tribesman attacked him and his friends and left them to die on a beach where the missionaries had landed to interact with the tribe. In the years following, Rachel lived with and ministered to the very people who killed her brother. Before she died, Rachel saw every one of them become followers of Jesus. That same tribe is now a "missionary village"—winning other people in their area to Christ.

What an amazing story of forgiveness—and of a woman committed to telling people about Jesus. The book of Ruth says of Ruth: "Everyone in town knows you are a virtuous woman" (3:11).

Be a woman of excellence. Tell others how God has forgiven you, and how He can and will forgive them too.

O Lord, you are so good, so ready to forgive, so full of unfailing love for all who ask for your help (Psalm 86:5).

This I Believe
My forgiveness may free someone
to accept Christ today.

Gazing at the Carpet

Max Lucado was right when he said, "We live in an art gallery of divine creativity! Yet, we're so often content only to gaze at the carpet!" That's so true. Look at God's wonderful creation...our hope for the future...the comfort of His Holy Spirit. These "displays" in God's collection are timeless, but the day-to-day pressures of living make us focus on the carpet...on the everyday happenings.

There's so much encouragement that comes from keeping our gaze on the Lord instead of the carpet. No matter what happens, remember: *God is in control.* Regardless of failed plans or whatever falls apart around us, Jesus absolutely promised to be with us to the end of the age.

Dear one, expect Jesus to be with you today. Live like it! Take your eyes off the carpet and focus on Jesus Christ.

> *[Jesus said,] "I have been given all authority in heaven and on earth. Therefore, go and make disciples of all the nations, baptizing them in the name of the Father and the Son and the Holy Spirit. Teach these new disciples to obey all the commands I have given you. And be sure of this: I am with you always, even to the end of the age"* (Matthew 28:18-20).

This I Believe

We live in an amazing world, and I will care
for the people in it in a special way today.

God's Billboards

What would God say if He could speak to us today? Of course, He *still* speaks to us through His Word, the Bible. But a recent billboard campaign raised the question in new ways. The posters bore messages that were signed "God":

"Let's meet at MY house Sunday, BEFORE the game!"

"Loved the wedding, now invite Me to the marriage."

"Need a marriage counselor? I'm available."

"What part of 'thou shalt not' didn't you understand?"

"I love you…I love you…I love you!"

"That…'love thy neighbor thing'? I *meant* it!"

Oh, friend, God *does* mean it. He *does* love you. And He wants to speak to you today through the Bible. Read His Word and listen to His heart.

The word of God is alive and powerful. It is sharper than the sharpest two-edged sword, cutting between soul and spirit, between joint and marrow. It exposes our innermost thoughts and desires. Nothing in all creation is hidden from God. Everything is naked and exposed before his eyes, and he is the one to whom we are accountable (Hebrews 4:12-13).

This I Believe
God's Word is my Life Instruction Manual.

Hagar's Answer

Have you met Hagar? Sarah was barren, so she encouraged her husband to lie with her servant Hagar to produce an heir. When Hagar got pregnant, she goaded Sarah about her barrenness. Years later Sarah had a son named Isaac. When Sarah saw Hagar's son, Ishmael, make fun of Isaac, Sarah demanded that Hagar take her son and leave.

When their water and food were gone, Hagar sobbed to God, "I don't want to watch the boy die" (Genesis 21:16). God heard her son crying and His angel called to Hagar, "Hagar, what's wrong? Do not be afraid! God has heard the boy crying" (21:17-18) Then God opened Hagar's eyes, and she saw a well full of water.

Maybe you've done everything you can to change your circumstances, to "fix" the problem, but there's no solution in sight. Dear friend, your heavenly Father hears you. Turn and "see the well full of water"!

> *Trust in the LORD and do good. Then you will live safely in the land and prosper. Take delight in the LORD, and he will give you your heart's desires. Commit everything you do to the LORD. Trust him, and he will help you* (Psalm 37:3-5).

This I Believe
I will not ignore the awareness of
God's direction in my life.

He Calms the Storms

My husband, Bill, and I were flying during a terrible storm. Lightning flashed across the sky. We were both terrified. Then I reminded Bill how Jesus calmed the winds and sea for His disciples during a violent storm. Bill prayed aloud, "Lord, You are the God of all creation. You control the laws of nature. You quieted the storm on the Sea of Galilee. Quiet this storm!" Immediately the rain and turbulence stopped!

Dear friend, the same power that quieted the winds and sea will calm the storms of your life. In any situation, make prayer your first response.

Jesus got into the boat and started across the lake with his disciples. Suddenly, a fierce storm struck the lake, with waves breaking into the boat. But Jesus was sleeping. The disciples went and woke him up, shouting, "Lord, save us! We're going to drown!"

Jesus responded, "Why are you afraid? You have so little faith!" Then he got up and rebuked the wind and waves, and suddenly all was calm. The disciples were amazed. "Who is this man?" they asked. "Even the winds and waves obey him!" (Matthew 8:23-27).

This I Believe
I trust God with my life,
so there is no need to worry.

Heart Transplant

Sheila became very bitter after her young grandson was murdered. She struggled to get up every morning and depended heavily on alcohol and cigarettes to get her through the day. One afternoon, Sheila discovered the *Jesus* video, a ministry of Campus Crusade for Christ International, in her cabinet. She watched the film and began to cry. At the end of movie, she invited Christ into her heart. She watched the video several more times. Her heart was filled with peace and joy, and her desire for alcohol and cigarettes was gone! Now Sheila loves to share the *Jesus* movie with others.

Friend, God is the greatest heart surgeon of all. He can take a stony heart and exchange it for a heart that is soft, pliable, trusting, and filled with love. Why not share God's love with someone this week? You can help them find Jesus and receive a new heart too.

> *Though I am surrounded by troubles, you will protect*
> *me from the anger of my enemies. You reach out*
> *your hand, and the power of your right hand saves*
> *me. The LORD will work out his plans for my life—*
> *for your faithful love, O LORD, endures forever. Don't*
> *abandon me, for you made me* (Psalm 138:7-8).

This I Believe

God will sustain me through
every event of my life.

The Heavenly Choir

Rick Husband loved to sing. He started singing in the church choir as a young boy. He also sang in school and community choirs during his teenage and college years. As an adult, Rick continued to sing. He once said, "I love to sing songs in church to tell God how much I love Him. It just feels great!"

Rick Husband was also the commander of the space shuttle *Columbia* that tragically exploded on reentry. Rick is now singing to Jesus face-to-face!

The Bible says that one day *every follower* of Jesus will sing praises to God in heaven. Oh friend, don't let anyone miss out! Make sure you know the good news of Jesus Christ and then share Him with people today. Invite them to sign up for the heavenly choir.

Be filled with the Holy Spirit, singing psalms and hymns and spiritual songs among yourselves, and making music to the Lord in your hearts. And give thanks for everything to God the Father in the name of our Lord Jesus Christ (Ephesians 5:18-20).

This I Believe
My songs are sweet sounds to
my heavenly Father's ears.

Divine Electricity

As a college student, Liz wanted to make a difference for Jesus Christ on campus. She started praying for her dorm neighbors and classmates and asked them for prayer requests. Liz also prayed for opportunities to tell others at school about God's love. She especially had a burden for one student named Jeff. He didn't seem interested in God, but Liz continued to pray. Soon Jeff started reading the Bible and asking her questions about God. It wasn't long before Jeff invited Christ into his heart! Liz was so encouraged to see his life change before her eyes.

Friend, when you pray in Jesus' name, you plug into the greatest energy source in the universe. Your prayer has the power to change lives. So don't be stagnant…take action and pray. It really is heavenly power.

> *[Jesus said,] "Have faith in God. I tell you the truth, you can say to this mountain, 'May you be lifted up and thrown into the sea,' and it will happen. But you must really believe it will happen and have no doubt in your heart. I tell you, you can pray for anything, and if you believe that you've received it, it will be yours. But when you are praying, first forgive anyone you are holding a grudge against, so that your Father in heaven will forgive your sins, too"* (Mark 11:22-25).

This I Believe
God is faithful and hears my prayers.

An Important Lesson

A college professor gave a pop quiz to her students. One conscientious student breezed through the questions until he read the last one: "What is the first name of the woman who cleans the school?" The student didn't know the answer. He asked the professor if the last question would count toward his grade. The professor said, "Absolutely. In your life you will meet many people. All are significant. They deserve your attention and care, even if all you do is smile and say hello."

Jesus cares equally for all people. Follow His example. Smile at someone who serves you today. Perhaps she or he will be a waiter, cashier, or bank employee. Tell each one how much you appreciate him or her.

By the way, the student never forgot that lesson. And the cleaning lady's name was Dorothy.

Since God chose you to be the holy people he loves, you must clothe yourselves with tenderhearted mercy, kindness, humility, gentleness, and patience (Colossians 3:12).

This I Believe
Honoring people is a way for me
to glorify God.

Kneading a Friend

Martha punched the bread dough roughly. Through her tears she cried, "Lord, why am I so lonely? My neighbors haven't even said hi. Even people at my new job seem to avoid me. What's wrong?"

After setting aside the dough to rise, Martha read Proverbs 18:24: "A man who has friends must himself be friendly" (NKJV). The Holy Spirit got her attention! She could use her bread-making to reach out to them instead of waiting for them to reach out to her.

Martha asked God to help her be more friendly toward her neighbors and co-workers. Soon she started a weekly Bible study where she served freshly baked bread and the Word of God to her neighbors. Her generosity helped people see God's love.

Dear one, God can use you too. Start today by being a friend.

The seeds of good deeds become a tree of life; a wise person wins friends (Proverbs 11:30).

This I Believe
God will honor the effort I make
to reach out to people.

Look Out the Window

Dave Brown was an astronaut on the space shuttle *Columbia,* which tragically exploded on reentry into Earth's atmosphere. He once said that former astronaut John Glenn gave him the best advice. John told Dave, "When you get up there, you need to make sure you look out the window." After Dave thought about it, he realized John was not referring to looking at the stars or the moon. He meant taking time to look out the window at all the people he cared about on planet Earth.

Friend, this is a reminder to us as Christians too. There are so many people on this planet who need to hear about Jesus. So look out your window today and think of someone who needs Christ. Then pray and go share God's good news with them. You never know what tomorrow might bring.

I solemnly urge you in the presence of God and Christ Jesus, who will someday judge the living and the dead when he appears to set up his Kingdom: Preach the word of God. Be prepared, whether the time is favorable or not. Patiently correct, rebuke, and encourage your people with good teaching (2 Timothy 4:1-2).

This I Believe
Every day holds opportunities to see the world with a godly perspective.

Mr. Ted

An executive's young daughter had tucked Mr. Ted, her most prized possession, into her father's suitcase for his business trip. She didn't want her daddy to be lonely. Mr. Ted was a ragged, well-loved teddy bear with two different button eyes and half its stuffing missing. It sat next to the father's suitcase while he went to meet with a prospective client.

When he returned to his hotel room, the bear was nowhere to be found. He finally found it covered with trash in the hotel dumpster. He rescued the bear and cleaned it up. Fortunately he didn't have to tell his daughter the bear had been tossed into the garbage.

Dear one, our heavenly Father loved us so much He sent His Son to a garbage-heap world filled with our sin. He rescued us from sure death and gave us eternal life.

> *He has rescued us from the kingdom of darkness*
> *and transferred us into the Kingdom of his*
> *dear Son, who purchased our freedom and*
> *forgave our sins* (Colossians 1:13-14).

This I Believe
I will tell someone today how Christ rescued me.

Don't Underestimate Prayer

It seemed like Linda saw police more than she saw her neighbors. The neighborhood was filled with drugs, prostitution, and violence. Linda invited other Christians living nearby to join her in regularly praying for their area. They cried out to God, and asked Him to perform a miracle. It wasn't long before the drug dealers moved out. Then the prostitutes disappeared. Soon there was peace in Linda's community.

Second Chronicles 7:14 says, "If my people who are called by my name will humble themselves and pray and seek my face and turn from their wicked ways, I will hear from heaven and will forgive their sins and restore their land." We hear this verse cited frequently to encourage prayer for our nation, and that is appropriate. However, we need to remember to pray for every circumstance where sin impacts our lives. Never underestimate the power of your prayers!

All of your works will thank you, LORD, and
your faithful followers will praise you. They will
speak of the glory of your kingdom; they will give
examples of your power (Psalm 145:10-11).

This I Believe
I will pray for the sinfulness I see
in my neighborhood.

Partial Obedience

The Bible tells the story of a husband and wife named Ananias and Sapphira (Acts 5). They were part of the early church. During that time, believers were committed to sharing *all* their possessions with one another. Ananias and Sapphira sold a large piece of property. Instead of giving all the proceeds to the church, he and his wife held back some for themselves. They *appeared* to be in full obedience when they brought the money to the church, but God revealed the truth. When the couple was questioned, they denied holding back anything. As a result, God struck them dead.

Their story is a warning for us today. *Partial obedience* is still *disobedience*. God wants us to follow *all* of His commands—not just those we think will suit our interests. Don't hold back—obey God *completely*.

This is the new covenant I will make with my people on that day, says the LORD: I will put my laws in their hearts, and I will write them on their minds (Hebrews 10:16).

This I Believe
Complete obedience to God's laws
is the goal of my life.

Sister Circle

recently completed a novel called *Sister Circle*. Although the book dwells on the lives of a fictional group of women, there have been many women over the years who've become like sisters to me. One of my co-authors for another book, Nancy Moser, wrote, "Women are special. We possess a unique, God-given talent (that men often cannot fathom!) to bond, to fellowship, and to share."

Friend, God has created you to be used by Him in someone's life. It might be your neighbor, co-worker, friend, or even a sister. You know who she is. Take time right now to pray for her. Consider ways to show you care.

I will sing of the LORD's unfailing love forever!
Young and old will hear of your faithfulness. Your
unfailing love will last forever. Your faithfulness
is as enduring as the heavens (Psalm 89:1-2).

This I Believe
God shows me His love through
my friendships.

A Sparkle Day

Sharon woke up feeling a little blue. Before she left for work she took time to pray: "God, I love You. I'm so grateful for all You do in my life. I know this is so selfish, but I could sure use some sparkle in my life today."

Her workday was well under way when the receptionist said, "There's a package for you." Curious, she retrieved it, opened it, and read the note inside from her friend: "I was thinking about you today." In the box was a fun, beautiful, jeweled watch—about as sparkly as they come!

I'm so grateful to God for the wonderful little surprises He brings into our lives. If He's placed someone on your mind to encourage, write her a note, send her a gift, give her a call…and do it today.

Those who are wise will shine as bright as the sky, and those who lead many to righteousness will shine like the stars forever (Daniel 12:3).

This I Believe
I can be the sparkle in someone's life today.

Together in Prayer

Dear friend, in our country we have the privilege to celebrate a National Day of Prayer each year. Fortunately we can pray this prayer anywhere, anytime.

Heavenly Father, Your Word says "Godliness makes a nation great, but sin is a disgrace to any people." I pray today for spiritual renewal across America. I pray that this nation will turn to You and seek Your will for this land.

I pray for our leaders, that they will live pure and holy lives and serve You in a worthy manner.

I pray for families. I pray for peace, guidance, and healing for those families who are struggling every day.

Dear God, for our youth, the future of this country, I ask that You will unite a mighty army of young people. Make them bold and steadfast in their faith.

In Jesus' precious name. Amen.

Upright citizens are good for a city and make it prosper, but the talk of the wicked tears it apart (Proverbs 11:11).

This I Believe
God hears my prayer for my nation.

Mission Hollywood

Karen Covell delivered a deeply convicting message at a woman's conference. Many listeners flocked to meet her...and apologized. You see Karen represents the Hollywood Prayer Network. And the women who met her asked forgiveness for how they had spoken against the people in Hollywood. Karen had given them a new, godly perspective.

To many people, Hollywood is a kind of foreign mission field. It's filled with people who are closed to outside influence. They need Jesus! Oftentimes they've been reared without godly influence of any kind.

Organized boycotting won't help. That can send a message of hate. Instead, pray for God to touch the people in the media and to send Christian artists to influence lives. Teach your children to pray for the people they see on the big screen too. We can make a difference in Hollywood...and it begins with prayer.

If you search for good, you will find favor; but if you search for evil, it will find you! (Proverbs 11:27).

This I Believe
God's love is available to anyone
who will accept it.

A Fresh Approach

In my years of ministry I've seen many creative ways for stimulating conversation. This method, called Soularium, is clever and effective:

- Offer someone a stack of 50 index-sized photographs.
- Each picture is fairly generic and contains no text.
- Ask her to choose three images to describe her life.
- Allow her to describe what each image represents.
- Then ask her to select another 3 for what she wishes her life was like.
- You then show three images to depict God and another three to illustrate what she can experience spiritually if she accepts Him as Lord and Savior.

This is a great way to begin a spiritual conversation. Go to www.ccci.org for more information on Soularium.

We can make our own plans, but the LORD gives the right answer. People may be pure in their own eyes, but the LORD examines their motives (Proverbs 16:1-2).

This I Believe
God will bless me with creative ways
to share His truth.

Backyard Mission Field

Sarah was rushing out the door to church when her neighbor Kathryn arrived on her doorstep. She had been crying because she and her husband were getting a divorce. Sarah's heart sank. She realized she'd been so busy that she'd neglected to stay in touch with her next-door neighbor.

From that point on, Sarah faithfully prayed for Kathryn. One afternoon she shared the gospel with her, and Kathryn received Jesus Christ.

Sarah and her family began to pray together every day for Kathryn and her husband. Kathryn's husband soon gave *his* life to Jesus Christ too! God helped them restore their marriage.

Dear friend, it's important to be active in your local church, but don't forget about the mission field in your backyard. Take the opportunity to pray for and care for your neighbors this week. They might be eternally grateful.

Those who listen to instruction will prosper; those who trust the LORD will be joyful. The wise are known for their understanding, and pleasant words are persuasive (Proverbs 16:20-21).

This I Believe

God's truth can bring healing to any situation.

Be Content First

Benjamin Franklin wrote, "A single man has not nearly the value he would have in a state of union. He is an incomplete animal. He resembles the odd half of a pair of scissors." I believe that's true! Oh, how many single women I know are looking for that "odd half of a pair of scissors"! They spend more time *searching* for someone to marry than they do *preparing* themselves for marriage. If you're single, here's a suggestion: *Concentrate* on your relationship with Jesus. Start with a daily study of the Bible. Get involved in a church group. I guarantee, if you're not content with your circumstances today, you'll never be content with them tomorrow. So stop looking for "Mr. Right" and start looking at the One who made "Mr. Right"—God!

> *I will exalt you, my God and King, and praise your name forever and ever. I will praise you every day; yes, I will praise you forever. Great is the LORD! He is most worthy of praise! No one can measure his greatness* (Psalm 145:1-3).

This I Believe
I choose to be content today.

Break in Routine

Sometimes a quiet time needs a bit of a break in the routine. As Hayley, a Campus Crusade staff member said, "Nothing can replace regular prayer and Bible study. But changing the routine can refresh my relationship with God and draw me closer to Him." She offers some terrific ideas:

Take a walk. Sometimes a walk away from distractions can allow you to focus more fully on Christ.

Read aloud or listen to Scripture. You can listen while you exercise, drive, or clean house. You can also sing them or pray through them.

Look through photos and remember times of God's faithfulness.

Friend, don't let your time with God grow stale. Balance consistency with variety.

I urge you, first of all, to pray for all people. Ask God to help them; intercede on their behalf, and give thanks for them. Pray this way for kings and all who are in authority so that we can live peaceful and quiet lives marked by godliness and dignity. This is good and pleases God our Savior (1 Timothy 2:1-3).

This I Believe
There are many ways to communicate
with my Savior.

Called to Send

In the good old days of pioneer missions, local missionary societies would wrap bandages and send care packages to faraway mission fields. Some of that still takes place, but there is a new kind of missionary support. Mission service is a *partnership* between those who go and those who send. Missionaries need financial partners and prayer warriors, to be sure. But they also need letter writers, cookie bakers, and encouragers.

So get out some paper. List everyone you know who serves as a missionary. Send each one a note asking how you can pray and how you can help. And then pray! Pray specifically. Ask God how you should help financially. And start helping! That's how the body of Christ works. If you can't go, be a sender.

Intelligent people are always ready to learn. Their ears are open for knowledge (Proverbs 18:15).

This I Believe
I can do something to help those who are serving as missionaries.

Selective Obedience

God commanded the Israelites to make sacrifices to Him. They vowed to give freely of their choice possessions and the firstborn of all their herds. Unfortunately, they strayed from that promise. They sacrificed sick and unfit lambs. They engaged in pagan rituals and rejected God's law. They *thought* they were still being obedient because of what they were doing, but their hearts were *far* from the Lord.

The tragedy is that we're often guilty of the exact same thing. Oh, we attend church, tithe, and read the Bible, but it's out of *habit* rather than a love for the Lord. Dear one, what you do begins with a heart for God. He cares about your *relationship* with Him most of all.

> The LORD rewarded me for doing right; he restored me
> because of my innocence. For I have kept the ways of
> the LORD; I have not turned from my God to follow
> evil. I have followed all his regulations; I have never
> abandoned his decrees. I am blameless before God; I
> have kept myself from sin. The LORD rewarded me for
> doing right. He has seen my innocence (Psalm 18:20-24)

This I Believe
My relationship with Christ will be
reflected in my actions.

Don't Miss Out

Annie had recently received Jesus into her heart. She said, "My old friends thought I was such a loser and now I was boring. But I determined to stick with God. I did and put everything into His hands."

Well, God gave her a wonderful new group of Christian friends. And Annie decided she didn't want a boyfriend unless he was dedicated to God. Annie joined a local church.

People often tell her what a positive influence she is. God has blessed her with a boyfriend who is totally dedicated to Him. They serve together in the same church. Now Annie's life is totally different. She says, "If you have never accepted Christ, you're really missing out on the mighty things God does."

Dear one, don't miss out on what God has for you!

The Kingdom of God is not a matter of what we eat or drink, but of living a life of goodness and peace and joy in the Holy Spirit. If you serve Christ with this attitude, you will please God, and others will approve of you, too. So then, let us aim for harmony in the church and try to build each other up (Romans 14:17-19).

This I Believe
The joy of my salvation does not
depend on someone's approval.

Fearsome Giants

How do you look at the fearsome giants in your life? Giants come in many forms—job loss, divorce, single parenting, maybe even public speaking. But they could be opportunities for God's remarkable deliverance.

On a trip to India, Julie was treated like royalty. Yet with that treatment came expectations. Wherever she traveled, people called on her to give a speech. One time she came to a village of several hundred people. Immediately, she was asked to speak. So Julie prayed about her giant called fear. After that, she rose and God gave her an amazing message to share. Julie saw that God was faithful as she faced her fears.

Take courage, dear friend. Our God is bigger, stronger, and more powerful than giants of any size.

Never be lazy, but work hard and serve the Lord enthusiastically. Rejoice in our confident hope. Be patient in trouble, and keep on praying (Romans 12:11-12).

This I Believe
I will face this day with confidence and hope.

Freedom Boat Club

Ruben and Rosemary were restaurant owners with a gift for good home-cooking mixed with Southern hospitality. They enjoy helping and serving others. The Solomons were their missionary friends who moved to the Sarasota area. Ruben and Rosemary wanted to help them. Because the Solomons frequently hosted missionaries, Ruben and Rosemary gave the Solomons a membership to a boat club, granting access to various boats to use for entertaining. Now they're "boat missionaries," using their membership for evangelism, and a place of rest for missionaries just passing through.

Friend, look for ways you can help those who serve Christ in your neighborhood and around the world.

> *[Jesus said,] "Watch out! Don't do your good deeds publicly, to be admired by others, for you will lose the reward from your Father in heaven. When you give to someone in need, don't do as the hypocrites do—blowing trumpets in the synagogues and streets to call attention to their acts of charity! I tell you the truth, they have received all the reward they will ever get. But when you give to someone in need, don't let your left hand know what your right hand is doing. Give your gifts in private, and your Father, who sees everything, will reward you"* (Matthew 6:1-4).

This I Believe
Giving secretly brings me great satisfaction.

From a Child's Mouth

Jacqueline prayed to receive Christ immediately after watching the *Jesus* film in Malawi. Although only nine years old, she spoke bravely the next evening to the crowd watching the film. Jacqueline shared about her belief in God. She said, "I can confidently say Jesus came into my life. He is with me now, and I feel I love Him so much. He can come into your heart too and give you the peace that He has given me."

No one moved to come forward. Some were afraid. Then Jacqueline boldly invited them to let God touch and change their lives as He did hers. And 407 people responded! The next night even more came forward to pray.

If God can use a child, friend, He can surely use you to tell others about His love. (Also, you can go to www.ccci.org for more information on the *Jesus* film.)

Such love has no fear, because perfect love expels all fear. If we are afraid, it is for fear of punishment, and this shows that we have not fully experienced his perfect love. We love each other because he loved us first (1 John 4:18-19).

This I Believe
The love of God gives me courage to
share my faith again and again.

The Gift of Your Time

recently heard a prominent sports figure say that she was "in recovery" because she bought too many things on the Internet. She admitted to spending more than six hours a day making purchases. She spent thousands of dollars on things she didn't need—and sometimes didn't even want.

This made me stop and think about how we spend our time—and how important it is to give our precious time to others. We've been made sons and daughters of God through Jesus Christ. And if we really believe that, we can do no less than give of ourselves to others—for His sake. And often to our amazement, we discover that the more we give, the more we're on the receiving end of God's never-ending, ever-flowing grace.

Remember this when you plan how you'll spend your time this week.

> *So, my dear brothers and sisters, be strong and immovable. Always work enthusiastically for the Lord, for you know that nothing you do for the Lord is ever useless* (1 Corinthians 15:58).

This I Believe

Every hour of my life this day is a precious gift from God to be used for His glory.

Give Thanks Always

For what are you most thankful today? Your family? Your job? Your health? Are you going through a trial right now that makes it difficult to be thankful? The book of 1 Thessalonians says, "Be joyful always; pray continually; give thanks in all circumstances, for this is God's will for you in Christ Jesus" (5:16).

Dear friend, our thankfulness should never depend on our circumstances or our feelings. Thanksgiving is an important part of our Christian lives. Before we ask God for material and spiritual blessings, we should first *thank Him* for who He is—our heavenly Father. God loves you and me… we should thank Him for that! So remember: Be joyful; pray continually; give thanks. When we make a conscious decision to do those things, it's easy to celebrate thanksgiving every day.

I will offer you a sacrifice of thanksgiving and
call on the name of the LORD (Psalm 116:17).

This I Believe
I can always find something
to be thankful for.

49

Have a Plan

don't know about you, but I like to have a plan. And if you want to be an effective witness for Christ, why not plan that as well? First of all, make a list of family members, friends, business associates, and neighbors. Then pray for these people regularly. Ask the Holy Spirit to prepare their hearts. During this next month, do a special act of love for each person on your list. Have a friendly chat on the phone, give a batch of homemade cookies, offer a helping hand to a busy mom, or extend an invitation to lunch. Pray for a clear opening that will enable you to invite each person to receive Christ.

"When God our Savior revealed his kindness and love, he saved us, not because of the righteous things we had done, but because of his mercy. He washed away our sins, giving us a new birth and new life through the Holy Spirit. He generously poured out the Spirit upon us through Jesus Christ our Savior. Because of his grace he declared us righteous and gave us confidence that we will inherit eternal life." This is a trustworthy saying, and I want you to insist on these teachings so that all who trust in God will devote themselves to doing good. These teachings are good and beneficial for everyone (Titus 3:4-8).

This I Believe
The Holy Spirit will precede my efforts.

Hearing from the Lord

Wouldn't it be nice to have cell phone connected directly to heaven? And anytime you needed to hear from God, He called you? You might even text or e-mail so God could send a personal message to you. While the "God phone" is an unrealistic dream, we do, in a sense, have a communication system from God. He's given us all we need to know contained in the 66 books of the Bible. No satellite or modem required. And we're blessed because the Holy Spirit doesn't need a cell phone…just our attention.

Hearing God's messages starts with your *relationship* with Him. Invest time and communication in this sacred friendship. I promise He will not disappoint you.

> *[Jesus said,] "You search the Scriptures because you believe they give you eternal life. But the Scriptures point to me!"* (John 5:39).

This I Believe
My friendship with Christ gives me
strength this day.

Investing for Life

Laura saw New York City as a mission field. When she arrived nearly 20 years ago, the Big Apple seemed like a spiritual desert. She met Kate, who wanted to begin a Bible study in her home. Then Laura invited Abigail, but Abigail responded, "I'm not interested in being in a group with a bunch of blue-haired ladies." But she came anyway. The group wasn't what Abigail had imagined! And God used Laura's insights to strengthen Abigail's faith.

Liz joined the group as a seeker. It wasn't long before she accepted Christ. Soon that neighborhood in New York City was blossoming for Christ. Now each of these women is serving the Lord in unique ways.

Friend, God has you in a strategic place. Plant the truth of His Word even if you feel you're in a spiritual desert.

I am counting on the LORD; yes, I am counting on him. I have put my hope in his word (Psalm 130:5).

This I Believe

I may wander in a spiritual desert, but
I do not have to stay there.

It's a Boy!

Wanda was so excited. She was expecting her first child! But during her sixth month of pregnancy, her doctor said there were some complications. He put her on complete bed rest. As her delivery time grew closer, things looked grim. The baby had stopped growing.

Wanda asked her church to pray. During their prayer meeting, they cried out to God. They beseeched the Lord for a miracle.

Wanda was at peace. She felt God had reached out and touched her baby. The very next morning, Wanda delivered a healthy boy.

Friend, God is our healer. Our prayers are part of His healing process. There may be someone God has laid on your heart today. Take a moment to pray for him or her right now.

Are any of you sick? You should call for the elders to come and pray over you, anointing you with oil in the name of the Lord. Such a prayer offered in faith will heal the sick, and the Lord will make you well. And if you have committed any sins, you will be forgiven. Confess your sins to each other and pray for each other so that you may be healed. The earnest prayer of a righteous person has great power and produces wonderful results (James 5:14-16).

This I Believe
Sharing my need with a friend and asking for prayer increases my faith.

53

View of God

Carol came from a somewhat religious background. She knew a lot of things about God, and most of what she knew frightened her. She viewed God as angry, distant, and unapproachable. The God Carol knew demanded more than she could ever give. She was convinced she would never be perfect enough to deserve His love or the heaven He'd made.

Then several people shared with Carol the good news about Jesus. They explained there is nothing she could do to *earn* His love. Carol believed her friends and eventually prayed to invite Christ into her life. She said, "I no longer picture God as distant or unforgiving; rather, I see Him as benevolent and very real."

Dear one, you may be a believer yet still not feel confident in your relationship with Christ. Ask God to give you assurance so you can live with certainty and encourage others to find the peace you have in Jesus Christ.

May the Lord lead your hearts into a full understanding and expression of the love of God and the patient endurance that comes from Christ (2 Thessalonians 3:5).

This I Believe
The love of Christ drives away my fears.

Over the Counter

I'd like to prescribe a little medicine that's good for the soul. It's over the counter. You can pick it up in any Christian Bible anywhere. If you're troubled today—relationships that are injured, a marriage that is struggling, a wayward son or daughter, a serious health issue—here's the prescription: "Look to Jesus." That's it. We all become weary and worn down because of the problems and pressures of life. But we don't have to stay down. We need to take our eyes *off* our problems and *focus* them on God, being dependant on Him for every need. Read through Hebrews 12 and fix your eyes on Jesus. It's the best medicine you'll ever receive!

> *Since we are surrounded by such a huge crowd of witnesses to the life of faith, let us strip off every weight that slows us down, especially the sin that so easily trips us up. And let us run with endurance the race God has set before us. We do this by keeping our eyes on Jesus, the champion who initiates and perfects our faith. Because of the joy awaiting him, he endured the cross, disregarding its shame. Now he is seated in the place of honor beside God's throne* (Hebrews 12:1-2).

This I Believe
I will look to Jesus today to
give me perspective.

55

Reason to Celebrate

Ashley was invited by her college tennis coach to attend an Athletes in Action Bible study. There Ashley learned about God's love. One night, Beth invited Ashley to begin a *personal* relationship with Christ. Beth joyfully described what Jesus had done for her personally. Well, Ashley prayed to receive Christ right then and there.

When she returned to the dorm, Ashley was greeted with hugs. The coach told Ashley this was the most important decision in her life.

Friend, you could be the one to help someone reach out to Jesus.

> Jesus told them this story: "If a man has a hundred sheep and one of them gets lost, what will he do? Won't he leave the ninety-nine others in the wilderness and go to search for the one that is lost until he finds it? And when he has found it, he will joyfully carry it home on his shoulders. When he arrives, he will call together his friends and neighbors, saying, 'Rejoice with me because I have found my lost sheep.' In the same way, there is more joy in heaven over one lost sinner who repents and returns to God than over ninety-nine others who are righteous and haven't strayed away!" (Luke 15:3-7).

This I Believe

The angels rejoice when a
person accepts Christ.

Pictures

Imagine using a set of 50 photographs to tell someone about Jesus. That's what two North Carolina students did on their spring break in New York City. Using a tool called Soularium, a tool that consists of 50 interesting pictures and five questions designed to easily flow conversations to spiritual matters, they went out to meet people and introduce them to Jesus.

They approached two college freshmen and a good discussion followed. They opened up about their lives and their beliefs. Then the conversation turned to God. The young women saw their need, prayed, and invited Christ into their lives. Since then, the four students have become Facebook friends, and the girls have joined the Campus Crusade group at their school.

Whatever way you choose, friend, share the good news about Jesus. (You can go to www.ccci.org for more information on Soularium.)

> *So we tell others about Christ, warning everyone*
> *and teaching everyone with all the wisdom God has*
> *given us. We want to present them to God, perfect*
> *in their relationship to Christ* (Colossians 1:28).

This I Believe

I experience great joy when I am privileged
to lead someone to Christ.

Stop and Pray

When Freida noticed that her neighbor Stella was frantically walking up and down the street, she ran to offer assistance. Stella's favorite bird had gotten loose. Immediately Freida prayed aloud, asking for God's help.

Before long Stella's bird flew home...safe and sound! Stella called Freida to rejoice that God had answered her prayer.

Friend, sometimes even the little things can bring God glory. As a result of Freida's bold prayer, Stella was drawn closer to God. Make quick, brief prayers your response to every situation. The next time you encounter someone in need, don't just say you will pray. Stop and pray that very moment. Think about what a wonderful testimony of God's love and power it could be. And most of all, it's an opportunity for God to receive glory.

Are any of you suffering hardships? You should pray. Are any of you happy? You should sing praises (James 5:13).

This I Believe
Trusting God to hear my prayers is
my first step of faith.

Stronger Than a Gun

Steve Fitzu is a former National Football League star and a Christian completely dedicated to the Lord. But it wasn't always that way. He was raised in a troubled home. Once, after his father, in a drunken rage, had beaten his mother, she ran to the kitchen and grabbed a gun. Steve's father picked up his young son and used him as a shield. In spite of such a troubled environment, Steve found unconditional love in Jesus Christ. He became a Christian at the tender age of 12. His parent's weren't followers of Christ, so Steve called a local church for help. He rode a church bus every week for years.

Friend, you probably have a child living in a troubled home near you. Make it a point to share Christ's love with him or her. When you do, you will change someone's world.

[Jesus said,] "Those who accept my commandments and obey them are the ones who love me. And because they love me, my Father will love them. And I will love them and reveal myself to each of them" (John 14:21).

This I Believe
Children can accept God's love
and understand His ways.

Teach Them to Serve

Julie said, "The greatest gift we can give our children is to teach them to serve." It saddens me that so many young people leave their faith behind when they begin college. I wonder if it's because they've been *served* instead of being *taught to serve*.

Julie and her two daughters spend holiday times serving needy people at shelters. Now in college, one daughter organized a Bible study and volunteers as a Christian camp counselor. The younger one uses her singing talent to impact her community for Christ.

Dear one, help your children honor Christ by serving their community, friends, and others. Teach them to ask, "How can I make a difference?" and "What did God put me here to do?" Discover together God's wonderful plan for your lives.

Paul wrote a letter to the church in Thessalonica and included some pretty clear instructions about work:

> *We hear that some of you are living idle lives, refusing to work and meddling in other people's business. We command such people and urge them in the name of the Lord Jesus Christ to settle down and work to earn their own living. As for the rest of you, dear brothers and sisters, never get tired of doing good* (2 Thessalonians 3:11-13).

This I Believe
My work will bring glory to God.

Train for Today

Oswald Chambers wrote, "It is the *process*, not the end, which is glorifying to God. His purpose is for *this* minute, not for something in the future." The Lord wants us to depend on Him and His strength—this very moment. Think about Jesus and His disciples. So many times the disciples were so worried about the "future kingdom," they forgot about fellowship with the Son of God now. They were concerned about who would have what position in eternity, so they missed the joy of spending time in the present. We're like that too.

My friend, are you concerned about tomorrow? Wondering how God will provide? Trust Him this very minute for your every need in the present. Don't let your assumptions or fears about tomorrow hinder your faith in the Lord today.

Those who know your name trust in you, for you, O Lord, do not abandon those who search for you (Psalm 9:10).

This I Believe
I will trust the Lord to guide my steps today.

Turn Your Eyes upon Jesus

Have you ever found something really valuable? Consider the man who found a dollar bill on the sidewalk. From that day on he kept his eyes focused on the ground. During his lifetime, he picked up 7 quarters, 11 dimes, 21 nickels, and 182 pennies. His legacy? A bent back and a miserly disposition! That's what happens when we keep our eyes focused on the wrong goals, when we're looking only for things of this world rather than for the things of Christ.

So what is your goal today? Is it merely making money or are you searching for the true treasure that only comes as you "turn your eyes upon Jesus"? And, as Helen H. Lemmel's hymn goes on to say, it's then when "the things of earth will grow strangely dim, in the Light of His glory and grace."

I will exalt you, my God and King, and
praise your name forever and ever. I will
praise you every day (Psalm 145:1-2).

This I Believe
I must keep my focus on Jesus.

Warm Socks

At the end of the summer, a friend began her first semester of Bible school in Wisconsin. Winter soon invaded the land, and she was unprepared for the chill. Temperatures were lower than normal that year and her feet were always cold. She prayed one morning for help in keeping warm. That very day, in her mailbox, she found a pair of warm socks. God was the only one who heard her prayer. And He had moved someone to answer this physical need even before she asked.

This is a simple illustration that can be echoed *thousands* of times by those who trust God for their needs. Our heavenly Father knows our needs *before* we pray. Our job is simply to ask Him and trust Him to provide. That's a heart-warming thought!

> *I love the LORD because he hears my voice and my prayer for mercy. Because he bends down to listen, I will pray as long as I have breath!* (Psalm 116:1-2).

This I Believe
God knows my needs.

Be Ready

My friend Judy was sitting next to a young woman reading on a plane. She asked, "Is that a Bible you're reading?" The woman replied that it was the *Book of Mormon*. Judy responded, "I enjoy reading my Bible as well."

"What's your favorite story?" the young woman asked.

Judy replied, "It's the story of Jesus and how He came to earth to die for my sins so that I might have eternal life with Him."

Only God knows the ultimate outcome of that conversation. He simply asks that we be faithful. The Bible says He promises to give the increase (see 2 Corinthians 9:10). Take every opportunity you're given to tell others about Jesus Christ.

> *God has given us his Spirit as proof that we live in him and he in us. Furthermore, we have seen with our own eyes and now testify that the Father sent his Son to be the Savior of the world. All who confess that Jesus is the Son of God have God living in them, and they live in God. We know how much God loves us, and we have put our trust in his love* (1 John 4:13-16).

This I Believe
God is honored when I share
the truth about His Son.

Contentment

Ruth sat at her kitchen table and prayed, "God, Shirley has a nice home, a better job than I do, and a husband who sends her flowers. All I've got is this shabby house, I stand on my feet all day as a waitress, and my husband doesn't even give me a card for our anniversary. Why can't my life be more like Shirley's?"

Then one day Ruth took a mission trip to Mexico. She saw homes made of cardboard and discovered that a family's annual salary was what she made in one month. Many of the women she met were widows. Suddenly her life looked much better. She prayed, "Thank You, God, for giving me these blessings."

It's easy to lose perspective when we focus on what someone else has. Look for the blessings God has already given you.

> *You want what you don't have, so you scheme and kill to get it. You are jealous of what others have, but you can't get it, so you fight and wage war to take it away from them. Yet you don't have what you want because you don't ask God for it. And even when you ask, you don't get it because your motives are all wrong—you want only what will give you pleasure* (James 4:2-3).

This I Believe
God is pleased when I am thankful
for what I have.

David's Tears

When I was young, most boys were told that a man doesn't cry because it showed emotional weakness and loss of control. A boy that cried was told he was acting like a girl. But in Psalm 86, David declared, "Be merciful to me, O Lord, for I cry to You all day long" (verse 3 NKJV). Would David's friends have told him he was acting like a girl? I doubt it! The truth is that our heavenly Father *wants* to hear our torments…the cries of our hearts. David recognized he needed the Lord's mercy so he opened his heart to Him. That was neither weakness nor loss of control.

Dear friend, if David's tears weren't offensive to God, neither are yours. Pour out your heart to God. Come to Him in your times of joy *and* times of sorrow.

Listen closely to my prayer, O Lord; hear my urgent cry. I will call to you whenever I'm in trouble, and you will answer me (Psalm 86:6-7).

This I Believe

Tears are a language God understands.

Doers of the Word

I've got a great suggestion today for your personal Bible study. The book of James says, "Don't just listen to God's word. You must do what it says" (1:22). So here's the idea: For one day or, better yet, one week, pick a verse and *do* it. For instance, we all need to practice forgiving as we have been forgiven (Matthew 6:12). So if you "do" this verse, decide that no matter what happens, you *will* forgive. When you are accused wrongly, forgive. When someone cuts in front of you in traffic or in the store, forgive. When your spouse or your children aren't perfect, forgive.

Is it easy? Not at all! God never promised us "easy." He did promise us the great joy of obeying Him. So thank God you are forgiven, and be a *doer* of the Word.

> *If you listen to the word and don't obey, it is like glancing at your face in a mirror. You see yourself, walk away, and forget what you look like. But if you look carefully into the perfect law that sets you free, and if you do what it says and don't forget what you heard, then God will bless you for doing it* (James 1:23-25).

This I Believe
God does not expect more of me
than I am capable of doing.

Don't Miss the Bus

Dawn and Cassie worked together in the World Trade Center. For several months, Dawn encouraged Cassie to invite Christ into her life. Cassie always responded, "Dawn, I know you're right, but I'm not ready to get on the bus." When the Trade Center was hit on September 11, 2001, Dawn and Cassie fled the building together just minutes before it crumpled to the ground. They ran down the street and jumped into an empty city bus.

Dawn said, "Cassie, I don't know if we're going to get out of this alive. Please don't wait any longer."

Cassie prayed to receive Jesus Christ into her heart.

Dawn and Cassie eventually made it home safely. And Cassie? She's grateful she didn't miss the bus!

Friend, take the time to share Christ with someone today.

When you produce much fruit,
you are my true disciples. This brings great
glory to my Father (John 15:8).

This I Believe
I must not take one day for granted.

Earthly Disappointments

At a weekly Bible study, Beth met Nicole, who felt guilty that the way she lived wasn't in line with what the Bible said is right. She wanted to change. So Beth showed Nicole an illustration to help her understand the struggle. She drew a circle to represent Nicole's heart. Inside the circle Beth drew a throne. She explained that either an "S," which stands for "self," is on the throne or a cross that represents Christ is on the throne. (See "Beginning Your Journey to Joy" at the end of this book.)

Nicole realized God wasn't the focus in her life. She prayed and recommitted her life to Christ. Now Nicole knows only God can satisfy her desires. No, dear friend, Nicole's not perfect…yet. But she's studying God's Word, and He is bringing about changes in her life.

How about you? Who sits on the throne of your heart?

It is by believing in your heart that you are made right with God, and it is by confessing with your mouth that you are saved (Romans 10:10).

This I Believe
God wants to be first in my life.

Garlic Christianity

There's a fascinating town in central California by the name of Gilroy, but it's better known as "the garlic capital of the world." Of course, every good chef knows the importance of garlic. It transforms the ordinary to the extraordinary. Well, the entire town of Gilroy carries that delectable aroma of garlic. You can smell it *miles* away. Whether driving from the north or south, you can't escape the smell of garlic.

This reminds me that, as Christians, we're to carry the *sweet savor of Christ* wherever we go. God's presence transforms our ordinary lives into extraordinary *eternal* lives. And those around us should be able to tell that a mile away.

Oh, you'll *know* when you're in Gilroy, California. Can people just as easily sense you belong to Christ?

Our lives are a Christ-like fragrance rising up to God. But this fragrance is perceived differently by those who are being saved and by those who are perishing. To those who are perishing, we are a dreadful smell of death and doom. But to those who are being saved, we are a life-giving perfume. And who is adequate for such a task as this? (2 Corinthians 2:15-16).

This I Believe

I will be a fragrance of life to someone today.

God Brings Good

Todd Beamer boarded Flight 93 to San Francisco on September 11, 2001. When the plane was hijacked, Todd and several passengers tried to overcome the terrorists, but their struggle ended in tragedy. The plane crashed in Pennsylvania. Authorities believe the terrorists were planning to crash the plane into the White House or the Capitol Building.

Weeks later, Todd's wife, Lisa, flew the same route to San Francisco. She wanted to encourage others not to be afraid of flying. She has continually meditated on the words of Genesis 50:20, where Joseph tells his brothers who had sold him into slavery, "You intended to harm me, but God intended it for good. He brought me to this position so I could save the lives of many people."

Todd's sacrifice probably saved many lives. And Lisa's example has given others strength and hope. Dear friend, remember that God brings good from evil for those who trust Him. I encourage you to trust God today.

Those who know your name trust in you, for you, O LORD, do not abandon those who search for you (Psalm 9:10).

This I Believe
Every challenge I face is an opportunity
to see God work.

God's Instrument

Okay, let's be honest. What's your reaction when a homeless person approaches you? When you're confronted by a teenager with strange hair? When you meet someone from another culture? If it's negative, my challenge to you is to respond differently.

You may be the means God has of touching that person with His love. You see, it's not enough for us to pray for people who don't know Christ as their Savior. You and I must be willing to *be* God's instrument. We should be available to be the means through which God reaches the lost and wandering sinners among us.

Take a moment today and pray for the strength and wisdom to be salt and light to the world by sharing Christ. God blesses those who are faithful to His call.

Do not judge others, and you will not be judged.
For you will be treated as you treat others. The
standard you use in judging is the standard by
which you will be judged (Matthew 7:1-2).

This I Believe
Someone needs my acceptance today.

"I Do"

"What makes your marriage work?" So many have asked the secret to my long-lasting marriage with Bill. We talked about that in our book *Building a Home in a Pull-Apart World*. In it, you'll find four steps that helped us in our 50 years of marriage. They'll help you too. Here's a brief summary:

First, *consciously* commit yourselves to the Lord and to each other. God established marriage as a *partnership*. Second, establish God-centered priorities. A vital spiritual life must be your main focus. Third, develop "other-centeredness." Be self-*less* in a self-*ish* world. Fourth, build a godly home for your family. God brings order out of chaos when you remain faithful to Him—and your spouse.

As the Scriptures say, "A man leaves his father and mother and is joined to his wife, and the two are united into one." This is a great mystery, but it is an illustration of the way Christ and the church are one. So again I say, each man must love his wife as he loves himself, and the wife must respect her husband (Ephesians 5:31-33).

This I Believe
God will honor my efforts as I do
something practical to
express my devotion to my family.

Jodi Takes the Cake

Campus Crusade staff member Jodi McReynolds has a knack for baking. One afternoon she prayed that God would use the cake she'd just baked as a ministry to others. That night, just before she got on an elevator, someone crossed her path. It was a young woman with whom Jodi had been talking about God for weeks. Jodi invited her to a birthday party and Bible study. Sure enough, God used that cake! Over pizza and dessert, the college student barraged the group with questions about the love of God. As they ate, they taught her about Jesus. That cake broke the ice!

Dear one, God wants to use you. He wants to use your gifts. Be available! Ask Him to use the chocolate cakes in your life.

Anyone who belongs to Christ has become a new person. The old life is gone; a new life has begun! All of this is a gift from God, who brought us back to himself through Christ. And God has given us this task of reconciling people to him. For God was in Christ, reconciling the world to himself, no longer counting people's sins against them. And he gave us this wonderful message of reconciliation (2 Corinthians 5:17-19).

This I Believe
Any expression of God's love
will not go unrewarded.

Lavished with Love

My husband lavished me with love every day of our lives together on this earth. I had the joy of being Bill's sweetheart for more than 50 years. But even more important than our relationship, is my relationship with Jesus Christ. He loves me more than anyone—even Bill! In fact, Jesus died on a cross so I might have eternal life. And that means I will be with Bill in heaven one day. And guess what? Jesus did the same for you! In 1 John 3:1, God's Word says, "See how very much our Father loves us, for he calls us his children." It is impossible to compare our human love with the all-encompassing, supernatural love of our Father God. However, I do believe our love for each other reflects our love for God.

Dear friends, since God loved us that much, we surely ought to love each other. No one has ever seen God. But if we love each other, God lives in us, and his love is brought to full expression in us (1 John 4:11-12).

This I Believe

God is glorified by my love
for my fellow man.

Never Destroyed

If you need a little encouragement today, let me remind you of an important fact: God loves you! That will *never, ever* change. Oh you may be fearful, even doubtful right now. Maybe you've been hurt or are unhappy. There will be dark nights and difficult days. But God is not about to let you go. You are forever His child.

Luke 12 tells us that God will not always shield us from anxieties or wounds, but He will give us the strength and courage to face them. I love the thought that our heavenly Father will mature us. He will use us effectively in His work in this world. Our faith in Christ may be shaken, but it will *never* be destroyed.

Dear brothers and sisters, be patient as you wait for the Lord's return. Consider the farmers who patiently wait for the rains in the fall and in the spring. They eagerly look for the valuable harvest to ripen. You, too, must be patient. Take courage, for the coming of the Lord is near (James 5:7-8).

This I Believe
One day Christ is coming back for us.

Never Give Up!

Even in the later years of our lives, God continues to fulfill dreams. We had just celebrated Bill's eightieth birthday, and he began to tell me all the videos he wanted to record. He presented me a list of books he wanted to write and a new ministry he wanted to launch. That was when he encouraged me to write a fiction book. Fortunately, most of Bill's dreams were realized before he graduated to heaven. Long-time dreams of ours came to fruition right before our eyes.

Dear one, have you given up on your dreams because of your age? You may think you are too young or too old. Opportunities are endless, and age should not keep us from stepping out and trying something we dream of doing.

Don't let *anything* hinder you from bringing people to a greater understanding of Jesus Christ. Remember, you are important to Him right where you are.

I can do everything through Christ, who
gives me strength (Philippians 4:13).

This I Believe
Nothing is impossible when I act in the
strength and will of God.

The Power of Love

How can you tell if someone is a Christian? The fish symbol on their necklace? A bumper sticker? The Bible says it's one thing: our love. John 13:35 tells us, "Your love for one another will prove to the world that you are my disciples." Believing love is important isn't hard. Putting love into action is another thing all together. Here are the ABC's of love:

> I *accept* you for who you are.
> I *believe* that you are valuable.
> I *care* when you are hurting.
> I *desire* only what's best for you.
> I *erase* all offenses between you and me.

Dear one, incorporate the ABC's of love into your daily life. That's how the world will really know you are a Christian.

You were cleansed from your sins when you obeyed the truth, so now you must show sincere love to each other as brothers and sisters. Love each other deeply with all your heart (1 Peter 1:22).

This I Believe
The Holy Spirit enables me to love
with Christlike love.

The Power to Forgive

It was April 20, 1999. Rachel Scott was eating her lunch on the grounds of Columbine High School. She was suddenly and brutally murdered. Instead of becoming bitter, Rachel's father, Darrell, turned to his heavenly Father for comfort. There he found God's love greater than any evil act. He found joy as Rachel's death drew many people to Jesus. He found the courage to forgive the two young men who took Rachel's life.

On September 11, 2001, many more lives were taken as a result of evil acts. Our country's loss was great. But dear one, each of us must run to the One who is love—Jesus Christ. It's there…at the foot of His cross…that we can find peace, strength, and the power to forgive.

Those who have harmed or offended us must also ask God for His forgiveness, but our forgiveness places them in God's hands. Turn to God today.

When you are praying, first forgive anyone you are holding a grudge against, so that your Father in heaven will forgive your sins, too (Mark 11:25).

This I Believe
Forgive me, Lord, when I harbor
unforgiveness in my heart.

Subtle Changes

have a spiritual warning for you today: Beware of the subtle changes in your world. So many Christian women have no problem watching R-rated movies or reading novels that have questionable content and morals. They follow soap operas every day and are absorbed by gossip magazines.

Friend, it's dangerous when you become too comfortable with the appeal of the world around you. When you open your mind to what the world calls normal, you weaken your Bible-based standards of holiness and righteousness. You see, "wrong is wrong even if *everybody* does it. And right is right, even if *nobody* does it."

Don't let the world squeeze you into its mold. Do right even if nobody else seems to be doing so.

We are instructed to turn from godless living and sinful pleasures. We should live in this evil world with wisdom, righteousness, and devotion to God, while we look forward with hope to that wonderful day when the glory of our great God and Savior, Jesus Christ, will be revealed (Titus 2:12-13).

This I Believe

I will resist the temptations of this world.

The Company You Keep

From the wisdom of Solomon, we're reminded of the importance of selecting the right friends. There are few more important lessons a parent can teach a child, especially as he or she approaches the vulnerable teenage years.

Charles Spurgeon wisely observed, "Show me the company you keep, and I'll write your biography ten years before your death…and I'll not miss the mark one in ten!" That's why the Bible reminds us corrupt company pollutes the individuals involved (1 Corinthians 15:33). The apostle Peter prophetically warns that in the last days "scoffers will come, mocking the truth and following their own desires" (2 Peter 3:3). The Living Bible puts it this way: "There will come scoffers who will do every wrong they can think of and laugh at the truth."

Make sure of the company you keep. Make sure of the company your children keep. Friends and acquaintances may impact our lives for eternity.

*The heartfelt counsel of a friend is as sweet as perfume
and incense. Never abandon a friend—either yours or
your father's. When disaster strikes, you won't have to ask
your brother for assistance. It's better to go to a neighbor
than to a brother who lives far away* (Proverbs 27:9-10).

This I Believe
My friends are so precious, and
I treasure their counsel.

The Decision

I've spoken to many college students who are anxious about their future. They have a burning desire to map out and plan the rest of their natural lives. That's a big decision for such a young adult to make. Oh dear one, if you're feeling the "pressure of the future" weighing heavy on your shoulders, you're not alone.

Rest in the fact that there *is* hope. Isaiah 30:21 NKJV says: "Your ears shall hear a word behind you, saying, 'This is the way, walk in it.'" Revelation 22:13 proclaims God is "the Alpha and the Omega, the First and the Last, the Beginning and the End." Entrust your future to *Him,* to the God who *controls* the future. Start today and get rid of the weight of the future.

> *Ever since I first heard of your strong faith in the Lord Jesus and your love for God's people everywhere, I have not stopped thanking God for you. I pray for you constantly, asking God, the glorious Father of our Lord Jesus Christ, to give you spiritual wisdom and insight so that you might grow in your knowledge of God* (Ephesians 1:15-17).

This I Believe
I have no reason to be anxious.

The True Comforter

Calvin Gooding got up early, as usual. He kissed his 18-month-old daughter goodbye. His wife, LaChance, was eight months pregnant and asleep on the recliner. She was experiencing back pain. Calvin kissed her and told her to try to have a good day. He went to his office in the World Trade Center. He never returned home. The date was September 11, 2001.

Since that day, LaChance has found strength in the true Comforter, Jesus Christ. Each day, she seeks the joy and sweetness of life only God can provide. She knows He has a special plan for her life.

Dear friend, how about you? Are you going through tough times? Tell God whatever is on your heart. Read the Bible. Allow your heavenly Father to wrap His loving arms around you.

All praise to God, the Father of our Lord Jesus Christ.
God is our merciful Father and the source of all comfort.
He comforts us in all our troubles so that we can comfort
others. When they are troubled, we will be able to give
them the same comfort God has given us. For the more
we suffer for Christ, the more God will shower us with
his comfort through Christ (2 Corinthians 1:3-5).

This I Believe
God's comforting presence is as near
as a whispered prayer.

What's Important?

God works mightily in the lives of women experiencing great trials. Jennifer is one example. Her husband had been diagnosed with aggressive brain cancer. He was gone in just two months. The great hole in Jennifer's heart left her clinging to God in desperate dependence. Yet the fragility she felt as a widow helped her be more patient with others. She said, "Unless we can display our wounds, others can't see the power of pain."

Oh, dear one, isn't it interesting that the *pruned* branch is the one that bears the most fruit? It's not babied or pampered. It's cut back and injured. Why? So it can bear more fruit! As the Bible says, "When troubles come your way, consider it an opportunity for great joy" (James 1:2).

We now have this light shining in our hearts, but we ourselves are like fragile clay jars containing this great treasure. This makes it clear that our great power is from God, not from ourselves. We are pressed on every side by troubles, but we are not crushed. We are perplexed, but not driven to despair (2 Corinthians 4:7-8).

This I Believe
The Holy Spirit will give me joy.

When God Says No

What do you do when God says no to your desires? A friend of mine was struggling with this. All her friends were married and having children. She wanted that life too, but she hadn't been on a date in months. Then God opened her eyes. She had been so focused on what God wasn't giving her that she was missing the many gifts He was trying to give her now. She decided to focus on what God was currently doing in her life at that moment.

Years later, when she and my son were married, Katherine left the single life without regrets. Is God saying no to your deepest desire? Do you long for a child, a husband, a better marriage? Dear one, fix your eyes on Jesus. Don't settle for second best when He has the very best ready for you.

I waited patiently for the LORD to help me, and he turned to me and heard my cry (Psalm 40:1).

This I Believe
God teaches me patience in very practical ways.

Be a PEST

Today, I'd like you to be a PEST to strangers. That's right, a pest. Here's what I mean. As you go about your day, be very sensitive to people around you, whether it be family, friends, or strangers. Look carefully at people and ask the Lord what they need. Some people will need you to offer up a *prayer* on their behalf. That's the "P" in PEST. You don't even have to know someone's name to pray for him or her. Second, you may need to offer an *ear*…to be a good listener. Others might need a *shoulder* to cry on—friendly comfort for their hearts. Some will need a tangible *touch*…or another type of encouragement.

Dear one, be a PEST God's way. Offer a prayer, an ear, a shoulder, and the touch of Jesus.

> *We urge you to warn those who are lazy. Encourage those who are timid. Take tender care of those who are weak. Be patient with everyone. See that no one pays back evil for evil, but always try to do good to each other and to all people. Always be joyful. Never stop praying* (1 Thessalonians 5:14-17).

This I Believe
God's grace can be seen through me.

Breaking Chains

Long ago there was a village blacksmith who boasted of his invincible strength. He proudly declared he could break anyone's chains. When strong steel links were brought to him, he found the weakest link...and easily snapped the metal.

One day the blacksmith broke the law and was put in chains. He scoffed at his jailers. Didn't they know his incredible power? Carefully he sifted through the links again and again, unable to find the usual flaw. In horror he realized he'd been bound by his *own* chains.

That's the way it is with sin too. You may think you're strong enough to withstand Satan's enticements on your own, but you're not. And when you repeatedly give in to temptation, it becomes a habit.

Dear one, what binds you today? Ask for God's help. He will set you free.

Thank God! Once you were slaves of sin, but now you
wholeheartedly obey this teaching we have given you.
Now you are free from your slavery to sin, and you have
become slaves to righteous living (Romans 6:17-18).

This I Believe
I do not need to fear bondage
while I walk in truth.

Chewing on God's Word

There is no better way to meditate on the Word of God than through memorizing verses. The Bible says to treasure biblical truth in our hearts. We're to contemplate Scripture, which gives us the "wisdom to receive the salvation that comes by trusting in Christ Jesus" (2 Timothy 3:15). Frankly, it's a bit like a cow chews its cud.

Have you heard the old saying, "Black cows eat green grass, from which is made white milk, out of which comes yellow butter"? That system's never been improved upon. The prophet Jeremiah wrote of Scripture, "When I discovered your words, [God,] I devoured them. They are my joy and my heart's delight" (Jeremiah 15:16).

Spend time today meditating on Scripture. It has the miraculous power to change your life. Let the Bible work its truths through you. That system's never been improved upon either.

Commit yourselves wholeheartedly to these words of mine. Tie them to your hands and wear them on your forehead as reminders. Teach them to your children. Talk about them when you are at home and when you are on the road, when you are going to bed and when you are getting up (Deuteronomy 11:18-19).

This I Believe
God's Word is a guiding light
in this dark world.

Drawing God

Years ago Art Linkletter hosted a popular television program called *Kids Say the Darndest Things*. While interviewing third-grade students, Mr. Linkletter found one boy with crayons in hand. He was seriously sketching a picture.

The host asked, "What are you drawing, son?"

Surprised his drawing wasn't obvious, the boy explained, "It's a picture of God."

Mr. Linkletter was reared in the home of a Baptist minister. He said, "But no one knows what God looks like."

The boy sat up proudly and announced, "They *will* when *I* get through!"

Isn't that the way it is with so many people? They picture God as *they* want Him to be. But no matter how hard we try, we *can't* make God into what *we* want.

There's one place to find the *true* picture of God—His Word, the Bible. Then, when you truly know Him, you can joyfully reflect His likeness.

You yourself must be an example to them by doing good works of every kind. Let everything you do reflect the integrity and seriousness of your teaching (Titus 2:7).

This I Believe
My life can reflect the attributes of God.

Fallen but Not Forgotten

The shadowy days after the terrorist attacks on September 11, 2001, were filled with fear and confusion. New York City residents were particularly affected. Campus Crusade staff rushed to the scene to help. New Yorkers—well, all Americans for that matter—were reminded that they are not in control of their lives. God became an everyday topic of conversation. As someone said, "Calamity clarifies."

After that tragedy, Campus Crusade distributed millions of copies of a wonderful booklet called *Fallen but Not Forgotten.* It honored the victims of the terrorists and provided a wonderful tool to talk with someone about the love of God. For those of us who have a personal relationship with Christ, one thing became very clear: We never know when we will no longer have an opportunity to talk to someone about God's love.

Please don't miss the opportunity to talk with those near you about the most important things in life—God's Word and His Son, Jesus Christ.

> *When God our Savior revealed his kindness and love, he saved us...because of his mercy. He washed away our sins, giving us a new birth and new life through the Holy Spirit. He generously poured out the Spirit upon us through Jesus Christ our Savior. Because of his grace he declared us righteous and gave us confidence that we will inherit eternal life* (Titus 3:4-7).

This I Believe
I will spend eternity with God.

Family Dynamics

This probably won't come as a shock to you, but I've never met anyone from a perfect family—my own included. My friend calls it "FD"—"Family Dynamics." You know what I'm talking about. The human family is marred by flaws and faults. All too often these are most visible in personal relationships and in the home. And sometimes it seems like those we love most do the most damage.

Before you consider someone unworthy of *your* forgiveness, think about how undeserving we all are of God's forgiveness. This may be very difficult to do, and I understand completely. But as you reflect on God the Father's love for you, those spiteful and ungracious circumstances may become an opportunity to portray His love to the other person.

Start your day by *choosing* to forgive, even as God forgave you.

O Lord, you are so good, so ready to forgive, so full of unfailing love for all who ask for your help (Psalm 86:5).

This I Believe
There may be someone I need to forgive today.

The Good News

Christ is risen! And that's *great* news! Jesus is a *living Savior*. He assures us of eternal life. He died on the cross in our place and for our sins. We are invited to have a personal relationship with Him. I call that incredible. So why are we so hesitant to share such good news?

I can guarantee that if I find an incredible bargain or if one of my grandchildren does something spectacular, I'm on the phone right away, sharing it with a friend. Aren't you the same way? Then why is it so difficult to speak up when we're talking about the greatest news ever—Jesus Christ?

Dear one, people *want* to hear good news and *need* to hear the good news of the gospel. Be open to sharing Christ today, and the Lord will use you!

I will praise the LORD at all times. I will constantly speak his praises. I will boast only in the LORD; let all who are helpless take heart. Come, let us tell of the LORD's greatness; let us exalt his name together (Psalm 34:1-3).

This I Believe
The good news about Christ is never dull.

Greener Grass

Incredible writer Erma Bombeck pointed out that "the grass is always greener on the other side of the fence. Trouble is…it has to be mowed over there, too!" Looking at what someone else has and secretly coveting it for ourselves is a deadly game for the human soul. We have no idea what heartaches and pain such an existence may bring. Comparisons are always dangerous. How much better to thank God for what He's given us. To be grateful that in His kind and wise providence He knows *exactly* what's best for us. Jesus Christ powerfully pointed out, "One's life does not consist in the abundance of the things he possesses" (Luke 12:15 NKJV).

In the final analysis, "the best things in life…*aren't things.*"

Then [Jesus] said, "Beware! Guard against every kind of greed. Life is not measured by how much you own" (Luke 12:14).

This I Believe

Earthly possessions are on
temporary loan from God.

Jesus Rocks!

Some time ago, a major news magazine showed dozens of happy teens with the heading "Jesus Rocks!" The story highlighted the positive influence Christian concerts, books, and movies are having on today's culture. It demonstrated the positive ways Christian products are affecting young people. Praise be to God!

And I agree. I hear reports of teens who are totally sold out to God and making an impact in their communities. The fact is, God's Word changes lives. And the teen years are vital times to deepen relationships with God.

> *Like newborn babies, you must crave pure spiritual milk so that you will grow into a full experience of salvation. Cry out for this nourishment, now that you have had a taste of the Lord's kindness* (1 Peter 2:2-3).

This I Believe
It is my responsibility to encourage the young people I know.

Keep Eternity in Mind

It was the early 1940s. Hitler was tyrannizing Europe, and the Nazis were killing millions of people in concentration camps. Sophie Scholl heroically resisted the Nazi regime, and her actions led to her death. Just before she was executed in 1943, she wrote: "People believe we live in the end times, and many terrible signs make such a belief all too credible. But isn't it irrelevant? Don't we all realize that, no matter when we live, God can call us at a moment's notice?" Sophie definitely lived with eternity in mind.

Friend, we *are* living in very uncertain times. But you can be sure of one thing: You have a glorious future if your faith is in Jesus Christ! Read the Bible every day, talk to God, and share His love with others. Live each day with eternity in mind.

The end of the world is coming soon. Therefore, be earnest and disciplined in your prayers. Most important of all, continue to show deep love for each other, for love covers a multitude of sins (1 Peter 4:7-8).

This I Believe
God's timetable is a mystery. I will live in anticipation of His return.

Measuring Up

Two boys were boasting about who was taller. The first little boy said, "I'm six feet tall!"

His friend laughed. "You are not! You're no taller than I am. How do you figure?"

The first boy responded proudly, "Easy. I took off my shoe and measured up my side...and I'm six feet tall!"

His friend scoffed. "Don't you know? You can't measure yourself *by* yourself."

And, my friend, we can't either. Life would be easier if we could. There are always people who are worse sinners than we are. But the only spiritual measuring rod we can use for a true measurement is Christ's perfect righteousness.

Everyone has sinned; we all fall short of God's glorious standard. Yet God, with undeserved kindness, declares that we are righteous. He did this through Christ Jesus when he freed us from the penalty for our sins (Romans 3:23-24).

This I Believe
Only because of Christ can I measure up to God's expectations.

Mincaye

Five missionaries headed into the jungle of Ecuador to reach remote tribes for Jesus Christ. They were murdered by members of the Auca tribe, who were known for their violence. That was quite a few years ago. Today that tribe is transformed by the power of God's Word and the life of Jesus Christ.

Mincaye (pronounced Mean-CAY-ee) is one of the tribal men who was involved in the deadly raiding party. His life is now given to Christ. He was in Colorado and spoke to the students at Columbine after the shooting massacre by two students in 1999. He said, "We used to live like you, killing for no reason. But now we read God's carvings and walk His trail."

Dear one, *that* is the power of God's love. Don't wait a day longer to tell those you love about Jesus.

> *The teaching of your word gives light, so even the simple can understand. I pant with expectation, longing for your commands. Come and show me your mercy, as you do for all who love your name. Guide my steps by your word, so I will not be overcome by evil* (Psalm 119:130-33).

This I Believe
The power of God can transform any life.

More Than a Paycheck

Amy had a burden for some of her co-workers. She began to pray regularly for them. Then she had an idea. She decided that while her co-workers fed their bodies, she could feed their souls with God's Word. She invited them to a weekly Bible study at noon. The response was so positive that it wasn't long before there were groups meeting four days a week!

Friend, wherever you work, remember your job is more than just nine to five. It's an opportunity to share God's eternal love. Pray for your co-workers. Look for ways to care for them. Invite someone out for lunch to talk about spiritual matters. Ask permission to host a Bible study at your workplace during lunchtime or after work.

Bring home more than a paycheck. Make an investment in eternity.

> *Don't be so concerned about perishable things like food. Spend your energy seeking the eternal life that the Son of Man can give you. For God the Father has given me the seal of his approval* (John 6:27).

This I Believe

My life can impact someone today.

No-fail Witnessing

Here's a recipe for succeeding: When you obey God and when you're motivated by love, you cannot fail. Even though your Christian witness may be rejected, when you share Christ in obedience to God's command, you always succeed.

I often ask people to memorize this phrase: "Success in witnessing is simply taking the initiative to share Christ in the power of the Holy Spirit and leaving the results to God."

Dear one, get hold of that thought. Write it down. This simple definition will help remove the burden of wanting immediate results. Whenever the fear of failure immobilizes you and keeps you from obeying God in witnessing, remember that you cannot fail.

I will send you the Advocate—the Spirit of truth. He will come to you from the Father and will testify all about me. And you must also testify about me because you have been with me from the beginning of my ministry (John 15:26-27).

This I Believe
I will leave the results of my witnessing to God.

Planes, Trains, and Automobiles

Jodi works on a college campus in Illinois. She also leads a Bible study there. One of the students was curious about Jodi's Bible studies. But because there were so many cults on campus, Karen was concerned this was just another one.

One day Karen mentioned she needed directions to the train station. Jodi happened to live near that destination, so she gave Karen a ride.

Plane trips, train excursions, car rides. These are great opportunities to tell others about Jesus Christ. Jody did just that. She shared with Karen about the love of God. And sure enough, two weeks later Karen came to Jodi's Bible study.

You never know what's going on in someone's life. God asks us to be faithful in telling others about Jesus. He'll do the work on their hearts.

Unfailing love and truth have met together. Righteousness and peace have kissed! Truth springs up from the earth, and righteousness smiles down from heaven. Yes, the LORD pours down his blessings. Our land will yield its bountiful harvest. Righteousness goes as a herald before him, preparing the way for his steps (Psalm 85:10-13).

This I Believe
God is preparing the heart of
someone for me today.

Pomegranates of Truth

Have you ever tasted juicy pomegranates? They have a wonderful flavor, but they are also so frustrating to eat! Each tiny seed is covered with a cell of juice. You can't eat a pomegranate without getting messy...but the taste makes it worth the effort.

Sometimes studying the Bible can be just like eating a pomegranate (but without the mess). You start reading a passage and notice it's hard to understand. You may pray, "Lord, what are You trying to teach me?" Then you start dissecting the verse word by word and discover the hidden sweetness. It suddenly makes sense. As the psalmist says to the Lord, "How sweet your words taste to me; they are sweeter than honey. Your commandments give me understanding" (Psalm 119:103-04).

Dear one, take time today to enjoy the wonderful truths of God's Word for you. It's worth the effort!

The very essence of your words is truth; all your just regulations will stand forever (Psalm 119:160).

This I Believe
I can live confidently based on the truth of God's Word.

Pray Five

Kit's neighborhood was full of disrespectful children, bad language, and loud music. She didn't enjoy going outside in her yard. She decided to pray. She prayed five blessings on five neighbors for five minutes, five days for five weeks. It wasn't long before change began to happen! Kit's neighbors started meeting her in the driveway and asking for prayer. Several neighbors received Christ. Some new families moved into the neighborhood, and Kit reached out to them too. Within one year, God had completely transformed the atmosphere of Kit's neighborhood. All as a result of prayer. Now Kit looks forward to going outside and visiting with her neighbors.

Dear friend, start praying for your neighbors. Try praying in fives: five blessings, five neighbors, five minutes, five days, five weeks.

Let all that I am praise the Lord; with my whole heart, I will praise his holy name. Let all that I am praise the Lord; may I never forget the good things he does for me (Psalm 103:1-2).

This I Believe
My prayers can impact
my neighborhood.

Praying Is Her Privilege

Cindy is a second grade teacher. She decided to start a prayer group at her elementary school. One morning a week before school, five teachers meet in Cindy's classroom. They pray for each other. They pray for staff members. They pray for their administration and their students. Cindy keeps a journal of all the prayer requests and God's answers. Each week they are awed to see how God worked.

The prayer group is growing. Four more teachers have joined. Through the power of prayer, there's now a special bond among these ladies. During a stressful day, one of them may whisper a quick "Please pray for me" to another.

Cindy has also seen God change her heart. She realizes now that teaching is her job, but praying is her privilege.

[Jesus said,] "If two of you agree here on earth concerning anything you ask, my Father in heaven will do it for you. For where two or three gather together as my followers, I am there among them" (Matthew 18:19-20).

This I Believe
Everyone needs someone to
pray with and for them.

Psalm in the Mirror

One of my friends struggles daily with the problem of poor self-image. It's hard for her to even look in a mirror. Oh, she knows God loves her, but she has a hard time loving herself. And that makes it difficult to share with others the good news of Jesus Christ.

The other day she told me of a plan of action that has helped. She's recognized God made her special, and He has a plan for her life. She repeats to her heavenly Father the words of Psalm 139 as she looks in the mirror: "I praise you God because I am fearfully and wonderfully made; your works are wonderful."

God does love you. He does have a plan for your life. See yourself as God sees you. He made you, and His works are *wonderful!*

> *How precious are your thoughts about me, O God.*
> *They cannot be numbered! I can't even count them;*
> *they outnumber the grains of sand! And when I*
> *wake up, you are still with me!* (Psalm 139:17-18).

This I Believe
I believe what God says about me.

Simple Math

What's one plus one? Does this seem way too obvious? But scripturally speaking, the answer is three! Jesus said, "Where two or three gather together as my followers, I am there among them" (Matthew 18:20). When a group of believers meets, the power of God is right there.

If you don't have a Christian group you meet with on a regular basis, start one or join one…a Bible study, prayer walk, or perhaps a breakfast meeting. I assure you, you'll never fully experience the great dynamic of the body of Christ until you're involved with a small group of Christians. As the Bible says, "Let us not neglect our meeting together… but encourage one another" (Hebrews 10:25).

We will no longer be immature like children. We won't be tossed and blown about by every wind of new teaching. We will not be influenced when people try to trick us with lies so clever they sound like the truth. Instead, we will speak the truth in love, growing in every way more and more like Christ, who is the head of his body, the church. He makes the whole body fit together perfectly. As each part does its own special work, it helps the other parts grow, so that the whole body is healthy and growing and full of love (Ephesians 4:14-16).

This I Believe
My life is enriched by my association
with fellow believers.

Sitting on the Inside

A little girl had disobeyed her mother once too often. She was told to go to her room and sit down on her "time out" chair.

Busy preparing dinner in the kitchen, the mother didn't check her daughter's room. Rather, she called, "Are you sitting in your 'time out' chair?" She smiled when she heard her little girl's honest response: "Well, I'm sitting down on the *outside,* but I'm standing up on the *inside*."

How much like us! We rebel against correction, don't we? That's why Scripture reminds us of the ultimate purpose of God's holy discipline: to conform us more into the image of His Son, our Savior, Jesus Christ.

Oh friend, remember to sit down on the *inside* and let God do His work in you.

> *My child, don't reject the LORD's discipline, and*
> *don't be upset when he corrects you. For the LORD*
> *corrects those he loves, just as a father corrects a*
> *child in whom he delights* (Proverbs 3:11-12).

This I Believe
I can accept God's discipline joyfully.

Stained Glass Windows

I t used to be that just about every church had stained glass windows. They were so beautiful and mesmerizing when the sun would shine through. The windows usually portrayed people such as the disciples, John the Baptist, Moses, and scenes in the Bible. These heroes of the faith would glow when the brilliant rays of sunshine passed through them.

When the sun shines through the colored glass it doesn't reflect the light. The light simply shines *through it* in wonderful colors and hues. Today, my friend, ask the Lord to radiate through you. Ask Him to let His Son, Jesus Christ, shine through you so that others will be captivated by His love in your life. Let your light shine.

> *You are the light of the world—like a city on a hilltop that cannot be hidden. No one lights a lamp and then puts it under a basket. Instead, a lamp is placed on a stand, where it gives light to everyone in the house. In the same way, let your good deeds shine out for all to see, so that everyone will praise your heavenly Father* (Matthew 5:14-16).

This I Believe
My actions today will show the light of Christ.

Take a Mission Trip

Allison sat glued to her television on September 11, 2001. She watched the tragic devastation caused by the terrorist attacks in New York, Washington D.C., and Pennsylvania. She decided she wanted to help, so instead of spending Thanksgiving with her family, she went on a mission trip to New York City. Allison and other volunteers swept, vacuumed, and dusted some of Manhattan's lower-income apartments. These apartments were engulfed in debris when the World Trade Center buildings collapsed. Through her work, Allison enabled many residents to return home to a healthy living environment.

Friend, God is pleased when we care for people in need. You don't always have to go far to take a mission trip. There might be opportunities right across your street.

> *Then the King will say to those on his right, "Come, you*
> *who are blessed by my Father, inherit the Kingdom*
> *prepared for you from the creation of the world. For*
> *I was hungry, and you fed me. I was thirsty, and you*
> *gave me a drink. I was a stranger, and you invited*
> *me into your home. I was naked, and you gave me*
> *clothing. I was sick, and you cared for me. I was in*
> *prison, and you visited me"* (Matthew 25:34-36).

This I Believe
I pray that God will use me today
in a practical way in someone's life.

You Can Make a Difference

When Sarah began her first year of college, she felt like she was the only Christian on campus. She was isolated and alone. Then she met some great Christian friends. Soon she and her new friends began praying together every week, and it wasn't long before there was a Christian concert held on campus and six students prayed to receive Jesus Christ.

Dear friend, God has a mission for you. Take time every day to pray for your neighbors and co-workers who don't know Christ. Pray they will open their hearts to God. Let God work through you.

We also pray that you will be strengthened with all his glorious power so you will have all the endurance and patience you need. May you be filled with joy, always thanking the Father. He has enabled you to share in the inheritance that belongs to his people, who live in the light. For he has rescued us from the kingdom of darkness and transferred us into the Kingdom of his dear Son, who purchased our freedom and forgave our sins (Colossians 1:11-14).

This I Believe
I have a mission today, and I will respond
positively to God's call.

20/20 Vision

When Fanny Crosby was six weeks old, she caught a slight cold that settled in her eyes. The family doctor was away. A man posing as a doctor prescribed a treatment that destroyed the little girl's sight. Instead of becoming bitter and resentful, Fanny believed God allowed this to fulfill His plan for her life. She became one of the greatest hymn writers in history. She wrote more than 9000 songs including "Blessed Assurance" and "To God Be the Glory."

Fanny once wrote: "If I had a choice, I would still choose to remain blind. For when I die, the first face I will ever see will be the face of my blessed Savior." Fanny had learned to see things from God's perspective.

Thank you, Fanny, for helping *us* see God with 20/20 vision.

I want you to know, my dear brothers and sisters, that
everything that has happened to me here has helped
to spread the Good News (Philippians 1:12).

This I Believe
My view of God is clarified daily.

A Shining Lighthouse

Jeannie keeps an electric candle lit in her kitchen window. While she's preparing a meal or washing dishes, it reminds her to pray for and care for her neighbors. One of the neighbors she prays for lives right next door. Fran was going through a difficult family situation. She was depressed and upset. Each week Jeannie visited her and shared God's Word. One day when Jeannie stopped by, Fran was smiling. She had received God's peace into her heart! Jeannie gave Fran a devotional booklet to encourage her new relationship with Jesus Christ.

Friend, pray for your neighbors. Look for ways to reach out to help them in times of need. These are dark and stormy times for many people. Be a shining lighthouse. Your neighbors might become eternally grateful.

God created everything through him, and nothing was created except through him. The Word gave life to everything that was created, and his life brought light to everyone. The light shines in the darkness, and the darkness can never extinguish it (John 1:3-5).

This I Believe
The peace of God is beyond
my understanding.

A Win-Win Situation

Pulmonary fibrosis. I remember the day the doctor spoke those two words. That's the name of the lung disease my husband contracted. Despite Bill's terminal prognosis, we ultimately responded with joy. Why? Because of two *greater* words: *Jesus Christ.*

In the book of Philippians Paul and Timothy wrote: "Living means living for Christ, and dying is even better" (Philippians 1:21). Our purpose for living is to have a personal relationship with Jesus Christ. As we grow closer to Him, our lives reflect His love more and more. Then we can show others how to have a relationship with Jesus too.

As followers of Christ, we know that dying is even *better* than living. Then we will see Christ face-to-face! Either way, it's a win–win situation. Eternity with Jesus Christ is our greatest reward.

> *If I live, I can do more fruitful work for Christ. So I really don't know which is better. I'm torn between two desires: I long to go and be with Christ, which would be far better for me. But for your sakes, it is better that I continue to live* (Philippians 1:22-24).

This I Believe
I will live today with
eternity in my heart.

Cheesecake

A Saturday trip to the supermarket usually involves stopping at a few "free sample" tables. One day, the man presenting a new line of cheesecakes never looked up. Head bowed down, he quickly cut the product into small morsels. Immediately they were snatched up.

Then something unusual happened. A woman came by, took a sample, and paused to say thank you. The man was shocked. He looked up with a smile and said, "Around here, we don't get thanked very often."

We treat God that way too. We take from His gracious hands and often forget to pause and say thank You. If a cheesecake demonstrator appreciates such gratefulness, how much more deserving of praise is our wonderful Lord? Take a moment right now to thank Him for all He's done in your life.

> We praise God for the glorious grace he has poured out on us who belong to his dear Son. He is so rich in kindness and grace that he purchased our freedom with the blood of his Son and forgave our sins. He has showered his kindness on us, along with all wisdom and understanding (Ephesians 1:6-8).

This I Believe
A thankful heart toward God shows gratitude to others.

Climb Every Mountain

Thirty-three-year-old Erik Weihenmayer climbed to the top of Mount Everest. That's an incredible accomplishment, but the feat is even more impressive because Erik has been blind since the age of 13.

How did he climb the peak? Erik's teammates each wore a bell on their pack. They shouted out instructions often. Erik followed the sounds and used custom-made climbing poles to feel his way along the trail. He literally put his life in his fellow climbers' hands.

Friend, that's the way we need to depend on God. "Trust in the LORD with all your heart; do not depend on your own understanding. Seek his will in all you do, and he will show you which path to take" (Proverbs 3:5).

Whatever decisions you have to make today, put them in God's hands. Listen to His leading. He will help you climb every mountain.

*[Jesus'] name will be the hope of all
the world* (Matthew 12:21).

This I Believe
Even the small challenges in my life
are important to God.

Cooking Frogs

George Barna, a Christian research expert, has written a fascinating book titled *The Frog in the Kettle*. Being from the Midwest, I understand the meaning of this title. When people cook frogs, they never put them into boiling water. The creatures would jump out. No, the frogs are placed in *cold* water. They're comfortable and unaware the cook is turning up the heat. And when they finally realize what's happening, it's too late. Barna's point is that complacent Christians fall prey to the world's comfortable surroundings. They're unaware that the heat of deception is ever increasing—until it's too late. They've given in to the world's clever appeal and the devil's enticing schemes.

Dear one, test the water you're living in. Scripture warns us to take heed, lest we slip and fall. Be aware of the temperature…and know when to get out.

Don't let us yield to temptation, but rescue us from the evil one (Matthew 6:13).

This I Believe
I will think carefully about the small compromises in my life.

Get into the Water

For many years Kim Linehan held the world swimming record in the women's 1500-meter freestyle. Her workouts involved swimming 7 to 12 miles *every day*. Someone asked her, "What's the hardest part of your workout?" She said simply, "Getting into the water!"

How true that is. Ask any writer and she'll tell you the hardest sentence to write is the first one. Sometimes our spiritual lives are that way too. We put off studying the Bible or spending regular time in prayer. But, friend, there is no better investment of your time than spending a few moments with God and His Word every day.

Jump in! Get your feet wet! Don't wait until you "feel like it." Start your day in prayer and reading God's Word.

I will exalt you, my God and King, and praise your
name forever and ever. I will praise you every day;
yes, I will praise you forever (Psalm 145:1-2).

This I Believe
Today is going to be a day for rejoicing.

God Will Make a Way

It was late one evening when Don's phone rang. His sister-in-law's family had been in a terrible car accident. Craig, Susan, and three boys miraculously survived, but their oldest son, Jeremy, was killed.

Don felt compelled to write a song to comfort Craig and Susan. Based on a verse in Isaiah he wrote, "God will make a way, where there seems to be no way. He works in ways we cannot see."

After the funeral, Susan told Don, "We've seen the truth of that scripture. As a result of Jeremy's death, many of his friends have received Christ. God really did make a way for us."

Oh dear friend, have you recently experienced a heartache or loss? Remember, God can turn tragedy into triumph. He will always make a way for those who trust in Him.

I am about to do something new. See, I have
already begun! Do you not see it? I will make a
pathway through the wilderness. I will create
rivers in the dry wasteland (Isaiah 43:19).

This I Believe
I will remind someone of the truth
of God's promises today.

Grow Up

One of our dearest friends had a 25-year-old son who'd never matured past the baby stage mentally. The joy of his birth turned to sorrow as the years passed. I can't help but wonder how God must feel when He sees *our* lack of maturity, especially after years of knowing Him. So many young women say to me, "Vonette, I want to be a woman of God. How can I make that happen?" Galatians says when the Holy Spirit controls your life, He'll produce in us "love, joy, peace, patience, kindness, goodness, faithfulness, gentleness, and self-control" (5:22). Now that's what I call growing up.

Like newborn babies, you must crave pure spiritual milk so that you will grow into a full experience of salvation. Cry out for this nourishment, now that you have had a taste of the Lord's kindness (1 Peter 2:2-3).

This I Believe

My spiritual nourishment comes from
the Word of God.

Health Update

Philippians 4 speaks of rejoicing in the Lord always. When my husband was informed he had contracted pulmonary fibrosis our lives changed dramatically. We experienced a mixture of pain, disappointment, frustration, joy, and great blessing.

There were times of encouragement and times of concern. No matter what, we enjoyed every day together and refused to complain. Our secret? We rejoiced in the Lord *always*. God was so good, and we saw tremendous answers to prayer. He is wonderful no matter the circumstances. We knew many people were praying for us.

Bill and I lived a lifestyle of rejoicing. Please join me in rejoicing always and giving thanks to our wonderful Lord for His daily promises and acts.

Always be full of joy in the Lord. I say it again—rejoice! Let everyone see that you are considerate in all you do. Remember, the Lord is coming soon. Don't worry about anything; instead, pray about everything. Tell God what you need, and thank him for all he has done. Then you will experience God's peace, which exceeds anything we can understand. His peace will guard your hearts and minds as you live in Christ Jesus (Philippians 4:4-7).

This I Believe
Rejoicing in the Lord will become
my way of life.

Helping Hands

Laura was struggling with breast cancer. She and her husband desperately sought the best of medical care. That required traveling to other cities for treatments. Laura was discouraged because she wasn't there for her children as much as she wanted to be. But the women of her church united to support her. Each afternoon a different woman would go to Laura's home. She greeted Laura's children when they came home from school. She helped them with their homework. She did the laundry and prepared dinner. What Laura couldn't do for her family, the "family of Christ" did through these women. Laura was able to relax and concentrate on getting well.

Oh friend, what a beautiful picture of the body of Christ working together. Look for someone who needs help today. Share God's love through your helping hands.

Share each other's burdens, and in this way obey the law of Christ. If you think you are too important to help someone, you are only fooling yourself. You are not that important (Galatians 6:2-3).

This I Believe
Few things are more important than being available.

How They Love One Another

"H ow they love one another!" When was the last time you heard that said about Christians? There's far too much conflict and jealousy in our personal lives and in our churches. Sadly, the unbelieving world scoffs at our conflicts.

Do you want to know how you can impact the world for Christ? You can do it right where you are. A story is told of a Navajo Indian woman who'd been healed of a serious ailment by a missionary doctor. She was impressed by the love he showed. "If Jesus is anything like the doctor," she said, "I can trust Him forever."

By faith, God's Word commands us to love. God's Word also promises that our heavenly Father will enable us to do what *He* commands us to do. It's our charge to "love each other" (John 15:12).

> *God showed how much he loved us by sending his one and only Son into the world so that we might have eternal life through him. This is real love— not that we loved God, but that he loved us and sent his Son as a sacrifice to take away our sins. Dear friends, since God loved us that much, we surely ought to love each other* (1 John 4:9-11).

This I Believe
The Holy Spirit enables me to love by faith.

"I Gave at the Office"

I'm sure you've heard the expression, "Sorry, I gave at the office." You may have said it yourself. It's a convenient way to tell someone you're not interested in helping. Unfortunately, I've met Christian women who have that attitude about their relationship with Jesus. They put in a minimum amount of time at church each Sunday and then, in essence, tell God, "I gave at the office."

God wants far more from us. He desires that we become more like Jesus. We're to put our lives on the line through loving and sacrificial action. We're to *constantly* demonstrate the hope and contentment we have in God and His love.

Start today. Look for someone you can help. Tell that person about your Savior. Being a Christian means you don't just "give at the office."

> *You must each decide in your heart how much to give. And don't give reluctantly or in response to pressure. "For God loves a person who gives cheerfully"* (2 Corinthians 9:7).

This I Believe
Giving of my life means more
than just giving money.

Known Before Birth

Expecting a child is an exciting time. The mother-to-be is sensitive to every movement of her baby. During the pregnancy, parents are encouraged to sing and talk to the baby. There are so many unanswered questions regarding that precious little life.

Now here's an amazing truth about the miracle of birth: God knows your baby even before he or she is born. Galatians 1:15 says, "Even before I was born, God chose me and called me by his marvelous grace."

Yes, the mother-to-be holds someone God knows everything about.

If you're an expectant mother, why not ask God for three things: wisdom in the dark days, patience in the long days, and love in the hard days. God will hear and answer your prayers!

You watched me as I was being formed in utter seclusion, as I was woven together in the dark of the womb. You saw me before I was born. Every day of my life was recorded in your book. Every moment was laid out before a single day had passed (Psalm 139:15-16).

This I Believe
God knew me then, and He knows me now.

Flight to Heaven

Dan was flying to Denver on Monday, September 10, 2001. During the flight, he noticed one of the flight attendants breaking ice with a wine bottle. "Isn't there a safer way you can do that?" he asked. The flight attendant was moved by Dan's concern. After some conversation, he gave her a gospel tract.

She said, "This is the sixth one I've been given recently. What does God want from me?"

Dan answered, "Your life."

A few minutes later, she prayed to receive Jesus Christ into her heart.

The next day, September 11, Dan read the names of those who had died on the two flights that were hijacked and forced to crash into the World Trade Center. The flight attendant he'd talked to was on the list.

Oh friend, share God's truth with someone today. We never know how long people have to choose Jesus Christ.

Don't brag about tomorrow, since you don't know what the day will bring (Proverbs 27:1).

This I Believe

I can be certain of spending eternity with God.

Leadership

What kind of leader do you want to be? Most people usually associate leadership with power and prominence. And there are some pretty egocentric people in leadership positions. But that's not what God intended for the church or His children. God insists we be characterized by our service to others. And we can do that at home with our children, as college students, or in our churches.

We serve God best by helping our brothers and sisters—wherever we find them. If we want to be leaders, Jesus says we must make servanthood a high priority. When we lovingly serve in that way—even without recognition or special appointment—then we become true leaders in the kingdom of God.

The greatest among you must be a servant. But those who exalt themselves will be humbled, and those who humble themselves will be exalted (Matthew 23:11-12).

This I Believe
I will lead by example.

Memorable Days

Do you remember when Christ came into your heart? Was it memorable? Can you look back and acknowledge that your life changed? Is the way you live still reflecting that decision? Scripture says that you were separate from Christ, but now you have been brought into relationship with Him through His blood shed for you on the cross.

Friend, if you can't recall recognizing your need of a Savior, please go now to Christ. Ask Him to come into your heart and change your life. What a momentous memory that will become. Recalling spiritual highlights in your life builds your faith. (Please read "Beginning Your Journey to Joy" at the end of this book.)

> *In those days you were living apart from Christ. You were excluded from citizenship among the people of Israel, and you did not know the covenant promises God had made to them. You lived in this world without God and without hope. But now you have been united with Christ Jesus. Once you were far away from God, but now you have been brought near to him through the blood of Christ* (Ephesians 2:12-13).

This I Believe
I will celebrate my spiritual birthday.

Mostly Blah

Is your Christian life more blah than joy? We're all guilty of getting caught up in our own busyness and, as a result, we neglect our relationship with God. Someone once said, "If you've lost the joy of the Lord in your life and you sense He's not near, who moved?" Take some time today to think about your relationship with God. Cultivate your bond with your heavenly Father.

Dear one, please don't allow unconfessed sin to pile up in your life. That creates a barrier between you and God. Be willing to change your priorities as you realize what is truly important. Share your spiritual discoveries with others. The very best witness is a joyful, radiant Christian.

[LORD,] you will show me the way of life, granting
me the joy of your presence and the pleasures
of living with you forever (Psalm 16:11).

This I Believe
A joyful spirit energizes me.

Have No Fear

Have you ever started talking with someone about your faith and they shut you down? It's a horrible feeling. Seeds of doubt are planted in your mind. The fear of rejection and the fear of failure will try to cripple your ability to tell others about Jesus. But you know what? Jesus saw His message rejected too. In fact, He was hated—even despised—for His teachings.

Jesus grieved, but it wasn't because His ego had been bruised. No, He was heartbroken because people rejected His great gift of eternal life. Did that stop Him? Of course not! And neither should it stop us.

Friend, start each day asking for God's help. Invite the Holy Spirit to guide you about when and where to tell people about the wonderful gifts of love and eternal life Jesus Christ offers.

> *When the Spirit of truth comes, he will guide you into all truth. He will not speak on his own but will tell you what he has heard. He will tell you about the future. He will bring me glory by telling you whatever he receives from me. All that belongs to the Father is mine; this is why I said, "The Spirit will tell you whatever he receives from me"* (John 16:13-15).

This I Believe

My fear of witnessing can be overcome with the help of the Holy Spirit.

Prayer for America

I t is so important for us to pray for our nation and our leaders. Join me in this prayer written by a former chaplain of the U.S. Senate, Lloyd John Ogilvie:

> Gracious God, all that we have and are is a result of Your amazing generosity. Since September 11, in the battle against terrorism, we have discovered again that You truly are our refuge and strength, an ever-present help in trouble.

> We rededicate ourselves to be one nation under You. In You we trust. We reaffirm our accountability to You, to the absolutes of Your Commandments, and to justice in our society.

> Bless our President, Congress and all our leaders with supernatural power. We commit ourselves to be faithful to You as Sovereign of our land and Lord of our lives. Amen.

God is our refuge and strength, always ready to help in times of trouble (Psalm 46:1).

This I Believe

The hearts of our leaders are in the hands of the Lord.

Recount Your Blessings

Remember the presidential election in November 2000? Weeks of recounts, court battles, and controversy about punch-card ballots and hanging chads filled the news. It seemed like it would never end! A billboard along a Michigan highway reminded travelers of those post-election days. It read: "Count your blessings. Recount if necessary."

Friend, are you feeling overwhelmed from a trial in your life today? If so, stop and count your blessings. Meditate on Scripture. Wonderful blessings and promises are laced throughout the pages of God's Word. We're surrounded with blessings from our loving heavenly Father! Praise Him for all the good things He has done for you. Remember how much He loves you. And when troubles come your way, count your blessings. If need be, count them two or three times.

The godly are showered with blessings; the words of the wicked conceal violent intentions (Proverbs 10:6).

This I Believe
There are daily blessings from God
that I don't even recognize.

Serving a Terrorist

Karen served meals that day as she always did—with a gracious and friendly smile. It wasn't until days later that she realized she had unknowingly served one of the terrorists that participated in the hijacked airplane attacks on U.S. soil on September 11, 2001. *Why didn't I share the love of Jesus with him? It might have changed his life and maybe even history,* she thought later.

Playing the "what if" game is a waste of time. God is in control. But it is *always* good to share the love of Jesus Christ. We're commanded, in fact, to do just that. And we can do that right where we are.

Fix your thoughts on what is true, and honorable,
and right, and pure, and lovely, and admirable.
Think about things that are excellent and worthy
of praise. Keep putting into practice all you learned
and received from me—everything you heard
from me and saw me doing. Then the God of
peace will be with you (Philippians 4:8-9).

This I Believe
I will live today without regrets.

Smiling Teddy Bears

I have a friend who loves teddy bears, and she has quite a collection. But here's an interesting thing. The other day she told me how hard it is to find a bear that isn't frowning. No matter how cute the outfit or comical the pose, it's rare to finding a smiling teddy bear.

Nehemiah must have felt just like my friend searching for smiles. The Old Testament prophet finished reading God's Word and shared its meaning with the people. He saw the joy in the words, but the people wept and mourned. He said, "Don't be dejected and sad, for the joy of the LORD is your strength!" (Nehemiah 8:10).

If Nehemiah sat in *your* congregation, would he have to look hard for a smile? Dear one, start today. Show the joy of the Lord on your face.

> *I will sing to the LORD as long as I live.*
> *I will praise my God to my last breath! May*
> *all my thoughts be pleasing to him, for I*
> *rejoice in the LORD* (Psalm 104:33-34).

This I Believe
I will choose to smile more today.

Taste and See

Every once in a while, I'll cruise past a cooking show on television. You may be a fan of Emeril and his "BAM!" style of cooking, but seeing food on TV just isn't the same thing as savoring it. In order to really enjoy cooking, we've got to *taste* the food. Place it in our mouths, chew on it, and relish the flavor.

In a similar way, Christianity is not a spectator sport. We can't just watch from a distance to get the full effects. We need to get involved.

Dear one, *taste* the Word of God. Read it, practice it, and do what it says. It will nourish and sustain spiritual life. When you've nibbled God's Word, you'll want to pull yourself up to His banquet table and feast. That's a meal you don't want to miss!

Taste and see that the LORD is good. Oh, the joys of those who take refuge in him! (Psalm 34:8).

This I Believe
Today I will dine at the
table of God's Word.

Things of Value

A friend recently told me, "Vonette, we know the cost of everything and the value of nothing." How true that is. We know the price of a new pair of shoes, but we take for granted the most important things in our lives. For instance, we get paper cuts and realize how much we really do use the affected fingers. Or even more poignant, we don't take the time to tell someone dear that we love them—and one day it's too late.

How can we get to the place of appreciating the value of important things? God's Word says to "enter His gates with thanksgiving." We can start by having grateful hearts for every blessing He gives.

Take a minute today to express thanks to God for the things you value.

> *When I look at the night sky and see the work of your fingers—the moon and the stars you set in place—what are people that you should think about them, mere mortals that you should care for them? Yet you made them only a little lower than God and crowned them with glory and honor. You gave them charge of everything you made, putting all things under their authority* (Psalm 8:3-6).

This I Believe

Everything God made is valuable, and
I will show Him my appreciation.

Take a Risk

When was the last time you took a risk for God? When was the last time you stepped out of your comfort zone? That you took a risk so God's purposes could be accomplished through you? My friend, God is eager to use you and me to work out His plans.

When firefighters went into the World Trade Center towers in New York City after the planes hit them (9/11/2001), they put their lives on the line to fulfill their "commission." They risked everything to save others. They rushed in where they were needed.

God is looking for soldiers and servants to bring Christ to a needy and hurting world—starting right in your home and in your neighborhood. Be courageous, joyful, and obedient to faithfully carry out God's commission.

So let's not get tired of doing what is good. At just the right time we will reap a harvest of blessing if we don't give up. Therefore, whenever we have the opportunity, we should do good to everyone—especially to those in the family of faith (Galatians 6:9-10).

This I Believe

There is true joy in meeting the needs of others.

Who Is My Neighbor?

The parable of the Good Samaritan in Luke 10 has always been a favorite of mine:

"A Jewish man was traveling on a trip from Jerusalem to Jericho, and he was attacked by bandits. They stripped him of his clothes, beat him up, and left him half dead beside the road. A priest happened to be going down the same road, and when he saw the man, he passed by on the other side. So too, a Levite, when he came to the place and saw him, passed by on the other side.

"Then a despised Samaritan came along, and when he saw the man, he felt compassion for him. Going over to him, the Samaritan soothed his wounds with olive oil and wine and bandaged them. Then he put the man on his own donkey and took him to an inn, where he took care of him...Now which of these three would you say was a neighbor to the man who was attacked by bandits?" Jesus asked.

The man replied, "The one who showed him mercy."

Then Jesus said, "Yes, now go and do the same."

Whenever we have the opportunity, we should do good (Galatians 6:10).

This I Believe
I will help one of my neighbors this week.

A Love Demonstration

Here's a lesson I continue to learn: how to love others. God continues to teach me in these wonderful years of maturity He's given me. He is showing me that loving *Him* is demonstrated by loving those around me. That includes my family, my neighbors, and those I work with. And that's true for you too.

God has chosen to relate His love to this world through you and me. Ask Him for the ability to put the message of His love into words and actions that will pierce the minds of busy men and women...and move their hearts to faith.

> *You have heard the law that says, "Love your neighbor"*
> *and hate your enemy. But I say, love your enemies!*
> *Pray for those who persecute you! In that way, you*
> *will be acting as true children of your Father in*
> *heaven...If you are kind only to your friends, how*
> *are you different from anyone else? Even pagans do*
> *that. But you are to be perfect, even as your Father*
> *in heaven is perfect* (Matthew 5:43-45,47-48).

This I Believe
I will show God's love even if it is difficult.

Act Like a Christian

George Gallup has been polling American habits and opinions for decades. And one sad fact he reports is that there is little difference between the churched and the unchurched. Divorce, infidelity, dishonesty—these things should not be in the church, but sadly they are. The Bible says to Christians today, "You must live as God's obedient children. Don't slip back into your old ways of living to satisfy your own desires. You didn't know any better then. But now you must be holy in everything you do, just as God who chose you is holy. For the Scriptures say, 'You must be holy because I am holy'" (1 Peter 1:14-16).

That's about as straightforward as it gets! Would someone near you be surprised to learn you're a Christian? Dear one, if you're a believer in Jesus Christ, act like one.

> Dear friends, I warn you as "temporary residents and foreigners" to keep away from worldly desires that wage war against your very souls. Be careful to live properly among your unbelieving neighbors. Then even if they accuse you of doing wrong, they will see your honorable behavior, and they will give honor to God when he judges the world (1 Peter 2:11-12).

This I Believe

Someone is watching how I'm
living my faith today.

Doing Something for Jesus

Many women have said, "Vonette, I don't tell others about Christ because my Christian life isn't that exciting." Is that how you feel? Do you need to get back into the Word, spend more time with God in prayer, and relight the fire you had for sharing the gospel? These words from Fanny Crosby's "We All Can Do Something for Jesus" are a great reminder for us!

A word to the erring, of kindness and love,
May often remind them of Jesus;
A song of our beautiful mansion above,
May lead a poor wand'rer to Jesus;
The acorn, when planted, though small it may be,
How quickly it grows to a wide spreading tree;
A lesson, dear children, for you and for me,
We all can do something for Jesus.

You are a letter from Christ showing the result of our ministry among you. This "letter" is written not with pen and ink, but with the Spirit of the living God. It is carved not on tablets of stone, but on human hearts (2 Corinthians 3:3).

This I Believe
I will reflect the joy of my salvation.

"Are We There Yet?"

How many times have you heard this from the backseat: "Mom, are we there yet?" The usual response is, "Not yet. We'll be there soon." That question comes up constantly on road trips. Children want to get where they are going *now*. I confess: Sometimes I feel impatient like those children. This journey of life is hard at times, and I look forward to the day I arrive at the final destination. I'll see my Savior face-to-face. And heaven is certainly sweeter since my dear husband went there.

Isn't it interesting that in the last chapter of the last book of the Bible, Revelation 22, Jesus said three times, "I am coming *soon*." Oh, like children on a road trip, it's hard to wait when we know something wonderful is just up the road. But be patient, friend. God has a wonderful place for us to enjoy at the end of the journey.

The angel said to me, "Everything you have heard and seen is trustworthy and true. The Lord God, who inspires his prophets, has sent his angel to tell his servants what will happen soon."

"Look, I am coming soon! Blessed are those who obey the words of prophecy written in this book" (Revelation 22:6-7).

This I Believe
Heaven will be a place of great
joy and laughter and love.

One Woman's Faithfulness

My husband had a saintly mother. She became a Christian at 16 and immediately determined to become a woman of God. She devoted her life to Bill's father and the rearing of their seven children. Today we sometimes hear criticism of women who find their fulfillment as wives, mothers, and homemakers. The popular thought is "There's something better." But dear one, it is such a privilege to be a mother—especially a godly mother. What a legacy Bill's mother has left for the world. Millions have come to know the Lord because of her faithfulness in Bill's life.

If you're a homemaker, you're making an investment in the lives of your children that will reap eternal rewards. Today's Proverbs passage is familiar to most people, but perhaps we should read it frequently to be reminded just how important mothers are.

She is clothed with strength and dignity, and she laughs without fear of the future. When she speaks, her words are wise, and she gives instructions with kindness. She carefully watches everything in her household and suffers nothing from laziness. Her children stand and bless her. Her husband praises her (Proverbs 31:25-28).

This I Believe

Today I will honor my mother and be thankful for the godly women God has included in my life.

Beauty

Did you know you are a prescription baby? It's true! God gave you a "custom design." He has *uniquely* equipped you. He has *specific* goals He wants you to accomplish for His purposes. Praise God for the wonderful and unique way He created your body and mind. Don't try to be like someone else. Ask God to show you the special and intricate attributes He created within you. Glorify God in your originality.

Oh precious one, He *longs* to show you the beauty He sees in you. Ask Him to reveal it to you today. I assure you, His reply will be ongoing.

> *You saw me before I was born. Every day of my life*
> *was recorded in your book. Every moment was laid*
> *out before a single day had passed* (Psalm 139:16).

This I Believe
The seasons of my life give me new opportunities
to express my God-given uniqueness.

Christid

Colossians 1 reveals how Jesus became one with us so we
can be one with God:

- In giving Himself, He made us members of
  His family and new creatures in Him.
- We experienced forgiveness of sin from our past.
- We received guidance and nurture for the present, security and hope for the future.
- We have access to all that Jesus is.
- God hears our prayers because He hears the
  prayers of Christ.
- God loves us in the way He loves Jesus.

Let me tell you, dear friend, this is something to get
excited about! This is the greatest news that can be shared.
Tell someone *you* know about God's love because Jesus is in
your life.

> *He has reconciled you to himself through the
> death of Christ in his physical body. As a result, he
> has brought you into his own presence, and you
> are holy and blameless as you stand before him
> without a single fault* (Colossians 1:22).

This I Believe
My excitement about my relationship with
Christ can be contagious.

Debbie's Plight

Debbie was crying hard; her pillow was stained with tears. Her husband of 15 years had just left her and their children to go into the arms of a younger woman. All Deb could think about was how she would get along. What would everybody think? How about the people at church? Would they understand?

Does that describe where you are today? Someone has disappointed you, maybe even rejected you. You wonder how in the world you'll be able to hold things together. Maybe you feel like quitting.

Dear one, the great news of the Bible is that you don't have to bear your burdens alone. That is what the church is for. That is what the love of Jesus Christ is all about.

O LORD, hear me as I pray; pay attention to my groaning. Listen to my cry for help, my King and my God, for I pray to no one but you. Listen to my voice in the morning, LORD. Each morning I bring my requests to you and wait expectantly (Psalm 5:1-3).

This I Believe
God will never reject me!

Depth of Desire

There's a huge difference between studying the Bible, and superficially reading it. It's a lot like comparing a bee with a butterfly. The butterfly flits from plant to plant, hardly tasting the blossoms. But the bee...it goes right down to the inside of the flower, even forcing itself into a bud only beginning to open. What's the difference? Most butterflies die in October, before the cold of winter sets in. But the bees stay safe in their protective hive. They've gathered enough nectar to last through winter's cold.

The same is true with us too. If we only taste God's Word superficially, we can't expect that when the storms of life hit, we'll be able to withstand the whirling forces. Dig deep into God's Word.

Taste and see that the LORD is good. Oh, the joys of those who take refuge in him! Fear the LORD, you his godly people, for those who fear him will have all they need (Psalm 34:8-9).

This I Believe
I will ask the Holy Spirit to give me a deep thirst for the Word of God.

Dust Bunnies

How often have you been doing some overdue deep cleaning and came upon "dust bunnies"? That little pile of dust and debris. It's amazing how quickly dirt accumulates.

Psalm 139:13-14 says to our heavenly Father: "You made all the delicate, inner parts of my body and knit me together in my mother's womb. Thank you for making me so wonderfully complex! Your workmanship is marvelous—how well I know it." God knows our strengths and weaknesses. I'm so glad He understands us and still loves us. It's hard to believe the God of the universe *chooses* to have compassion for us... for these "piles of dust"...mere "dust bunnies"...that walk the earth.

Dear one, He *does* care!

> *The LORD is like a father to his children, tender and compassionate to those who fear him. For he knows how weak we are; he remembers we are only dust* (Psalm 103:13-14).

This I Believe

When I feel "dusty," I know God sees me as clean.

A Tribute to Fathers

William and Morrow were a happy couple starting out life together. He was a successful businessman and farmer. She chose to stay home and raise their four children. William felt a call from God to preach, but it never seemed to work out...until the day their firstborn son entered ministry. William said, "I prayed for years for a way to be opened to minister. My heart burned, and I wondered why God didn't answer my prayer. Now I believe my part was to raise a son to be a preacher." These words are from William Franklin Graham, Senior—Billy Graham's father.

Dear one, your greatest calling is to be a loving mother for your children. Pray for them. Ask God to give you the wisdom to lead them into a relationship with Jesus Christ.

You must love the LORD your God with all your heart, all your soul, and all your strength. And you must commit yourselves wholeheartedly to these commands that I am giving you today. Repeat them again and again to your children. Talk about them when you are at home and when you are on the road, when you are going to bed and when you are getting up (Deuteronomy 6:4-7).

This I Believe

I can influence a child today by the words I say.

God Is in Control

My friend, don't underestimate what God wants to do in your life. And don't be surprised at how, even in your weakness, when you're fully committed to Him He'll do marvelous things for His glory. Vance Havner, a country preacher of another era, said, "So many Christians live such subnormal lives that when they see what's 'normal,' they think it's abnormal."

The only requirement God places on you is that you be faithful. That you put aside your agenda and make His a priority. God has a perfect plan for your life. True, you may not always understand God's work on this earth. But you know what? It's not important that you always comprehend. Be encouraged and remember: "God is in control!"

So you have not received a spirit that makes you fearful slaves. Instead, you received God's Spirit when he adopted you as his own children. Now we call him, "Abba, Father." For his Spirit joins with our spirit to affirm that we are God's children (Romans 8:15-16).

This I Believe
Living as God's child is a freeing experience.

What Is Prayer-walking?

What do you think of when you hear the term "prayer-walking"? Do you imagine standing in front of your neighbor's house praying with raised hands? Maybe shouting hallelujah? Or perhaps kneeling in their driveways with your hands folded?

It's not that at all. Think of prayer-walking as being on the scene…without making one. It's quietly praying for the people in the houses as you walk through your neighborhood. It's asking God to bless each family. If you know of specific needs, you pray for those too. You ask God to fill your neighbors with joy. And if they don't know Christ, you ask Him to touch their lives and pray they'll soon meet Him.

Why not start prayer-walking your neighborhood this week? It's a great way to get in shape physically and spiritually. As for your neighbors—their lives may be changed forever.

> *This same Good News that came to you is going out all over the world. It is bearing fruit everywhere by changing lives, just as it changed your lives from the day you first heard and understood the truth about God's wonderful grace* (Colossians 1:6).

This I Believe

My prayers are a powerful force for good.

149

Prayer Power

Helen lived in a quiet neighborhood. However, things began to change when one house became a rental. Drugs and prostitution arrived. Soon several homeowners moved away. More drug dealers moved in. Helen was continuously calling the police. She despairingly watched her community become a place of darkness.

Then God impressed her to take spiritual action. Helen started prayer-walking her neighborhood. She prayed that God would perform a miracle on her street. It wasn't long before the drugs and the prostitution disappeared. Peace returned.

Dear friend, throughout history, God has revealed His mighty power through prayer. And that same power is available to help you with your daily problems. When you feel weak and limited, don't despair. Pray and ask God for help. Tap into His power supply.

The LORD rules over the floodwaters. The Lord reigns as king forever. The LORD gives his people strength. The LORD blesses them with peace (Psalm 29:10-11).

This I Believe
I will boldly step out and pray
over my circumstances.

Money's Limitations

In these days of economic slowdowns and job layoffs, it's good to remember the value God places on money. The poorest person in the world isn't someone who's gone bankrupt. No, it's the person who is without God and, consequently, without hope.

Some years ago, the editors of *The Wall Street Journal* made a powerful statement: "Money is the article which may be used as a universal passport to *everywhere*, except heaven, and the universal provider of *everything* except…happiness." And they're right! You see, as Christians our happiness is centered on our personal relationship with God through our Lord Jesus Christ.

> *"Teacher, please tell my brother to divide*
> *our father's estate with me."*
>
> *Jesus replied, "Friend, who made me a judge over you*
> *to decide such things as that?" Then he said, "Beware!*
> *Guard against every kind of greed. Life is not*
> *measured by how much you own"* (Luke 12:13-15).

This I Believe
I will enjoy my possessions, but
I will not let them possess me.

God Does What He Says

Do we really trust God to do what He says He will do? If we truly believe that, the wonderful blessings He promises will be ours. And that applies to every area of our lives!

Are you struggling to make ends meet? If you're a mother, do you need more patience? Perhaps you're frustrated with your teenager or possibly your husband's long hours at work?

Dear friend, there's not a single circumstance you face that is beyond God's ability to control. He will meet your every need of heart and life. Expect a great blessing from Him today. Why? Because He does what He says. What a wonderful truth to share with others.

I know how to live on almost nothing or with everything. I have learned the secret of living in every situation, whether it is with a full stomach or empty, with plenty or little. For I can do everything through Christ, who gives me strength (Philippians 4:12-13).

This I Believe
I will remember the many times God
has kept His word in my life.

Heroes in Short Supply

A poll I read recently said 70 percent of Americans have no hero. What a shame. And, unfortunately, what heroes we *do* have are mostly athletes and actors. Why not set today aside to honor *real* heroes? Those who paid the ultimate price for our freedom. Those whose sacrifices made possible our free exercise of religion.

I thank God for this wonderful country of ours. I thank Him for the men and women who placed their lives on the line so we can worship our heavenly Father openly. So many Christians around the world live in fear of arrest, torture, and even death for their beliefs.

Dear one, never lose sight of this precious gift of freedom that has been given to us at the high cost of so many lives.

I will praise you, LORD, with all my heart; I will tell of all the marvelous things you have done. I will be filled with joy because of you. I will sing praises to your name, O Most High (Psalm 9:1-2).

This I Believe
I will tell someone today how privileged
I feel to live in a nation that
honors religious freedom.

Have You Been Robbed?

Dear friend, are you stressed? Burned out? Confused as to what God wants you to do? I'm afraid to say that you may very well have been robbed! Robbed of an intimate relationship with God. One of the greatest hindrances to spiritual growth is busyness. Oh how often we dismiss quiet times with Jesus because we are too rushed or too tired. Experiencing God's presence is the *greatest* privilege a believer is given. But it comes only as we spend *time* with Him in prayer and Bible study.

The psalmist tells over and over how his time with the Lord and His Word revived his soul and gave him joy. Dear one, don't lose the amazing opportunity you have in this life. Schedule time with the Lord today. You will *not* be disappointed!

> *Let the godly rejoice. Let them be glad in God's presence. Let them be filled with joy. Sing praises to God and to his name! Sing loud praises to him who rides the clouds. His name is the LORD— rejoice in his presence!* (Psalm 68:3-4).

This I Believe

I will schedule a specific time to read God's Word and pray...and then do it.

Listen

Do you remember that God created the heavens and the earth in six days? After each day's creation He said, "It is good." And He was pleased with what He had done. Then He created man and later said, "It is not good for the man to be alone." And then He created woman to be a helpmate, a partner. Do you know why He created her last? Because He didn't want her telling Him how to create everything else!

Oh, dear friend, God did create you to be a helpmate… a *partner*. You need to be listened to and heard, but you also need to take time to listen to your husband if you're married. The Bible says a gentle and quiet spirit has unfading beauty and is of great worth in God's sight (1 Peter 3:4).

Listen more today. You might be amazed at what you hear.

If you want to enjoy life and see many happy days, keep your tongue from speaking evil and your lips from telling lies. Turn away from evil and do good. Search for peace, and work to maintain it (1 Peter 3:10-11).

This I Believe
The Holy Spirit will help me
control my tongue.

A Tribute to Mothers

Little Tommy came home from school in tears. His teacher had written another note. His mother opened the letter and read the teacher's rather harsh words: "Your child is dumb. We can't do anything for him." Tommy's mother wrote back, "You don't understand my boy. I will teach him myself."

Sometimes the love of a mother overcomes the obstacles our culture says are too great. That was true for Tommy. His mother *did* teach her son—and you know him as Thomas Alva Edison, one of the greatest inventors of our time.

Never underestimate the power of your love and dedication to your children. The world may say they have shortcomings, but your influence is profound. God designed you to provide just what your children need. Ask Him to help you mold them into the leaders of the future.

Children are a gift from the LORD; they are
a reward from him (Psalm 127:3).

This I Believe
My investment in the lives of children
holds great rewards.

Who Is Your Intercessor?

Attorneys have a familiar saying: "A person who serves as his own attorney has a *fool* for a client." Well, I'm grateful for my many friends who are legal counselors. Their lives are dedicated to helping people understand complicated laws. But when it comes to eternity, to standing before God, many people have foolishly decided they don't need an intercessor. They think they can represent themselves. They tell themselves, *Maybe I'm not good enough to go to heaven, but I'm certainly not bad enough to go to hell.*

But the fact is that it's not *their* opinion or even *our* opinion that matters. It's God's heaven and, according to Jesus, there's only one way to get there—through personal faith in Him. He said, "I am the way, the truth, and the life. No one can come to the Father except through me" (John 14:6).

So don't be foolish, trying in your own goodness to represent yourself before God. Trust in the Wonderful Counselor Jesus Christ.

I know the greatness of the LORD—that our Lord is greater than any other god. The LORD does whatever pleases him throughout all heaven and earth, and on the seas and in their depths (Psalm 135:5-6).

This I Believe
I know that God is just and He will always treat me fairly.

Reporting the Good News

Sharon was a journalism student in college when she received Christ. She felt called to become a missionary. God showed her a different plan at a Campus Crusade for Christ discipleship conference.

During that week, my husband, Bill, challenged her to be an ambassador for Christ in the secular media. Today Sharon is a religion editor at a major press organization in Washington, D.C. In her job, she objectively reports the news to her audience. But she also looks for opportunities to share God's good news. As a result, Sharon's co-workers ask for prayer when they're going through difficulties.

Friend, if you're in the secular workplace, shine as a light for God. Pray for your co-workers. Look for opportunities to share God's truth. There's a mission field right before your eyes.

*Just as you sent me into the world, I am sending
them into the world. And I give myself as a
holy sacrifice for them so they can be made
holy by your truth* (John 17:18-19).

This I Believe
Someone I meet today needs
to be encouraged.

"Shy Bearing" Plants

People growing up in Oklahoma know that farmers call certain plants "shy bearers." It's a description of trees or vines that have just enough fruit to determine what they are, but *not* enough to be of any value in the harvest. Unfortunately, when it comes to serving the Lord, there are some who are best described as shy bearers. People know they're Christians; however, it's difficult to see much fruit of the Holy Spirit in their lives.

I think that's exactly what Jesus meant when He said, "My Father is the gardener. He cuts off every branch of mine that doesn't produce fruit, and he prunes the branches that do bear fruit so they will produce even more" (John 15:1-2). "More" is the operative word.

God doesn't want you to be a shy bearer. He wants you to produce rich, abundant fruit.

> *[Jesus said,] "If you remain in me and my words remain in you, you may ask for anything you want, and it will be granted! When you produce much fruit, you are my true disciples. This brings great glory to my Father"* (John 15:7-8).

This I Believe

I can bear fruit at any stage of life.

Put Your Feet in Motion

Tanya and Kathy were prayer-walking through a neighborhood. Suddenly a young woman named Deborah ran across her yard to meet them. Tanya asked Deborah if they could pray for her. Deborah replied that she had just asked God to send someone to tell her about Jesus! Then Deborah called out to her friend Gracie so she could hear about Jesus too.

Tanya and Kathy explained how to enter into a personal relationship with God. Deborah and Gracie bowed their heads and invited Jesus Christ into their hearts on the spot.

Friend, think of one person you know who needs to hear about Christ. Then put your feet into motion and go and share the good news.

> *How can they call on him to save them unless they*
> *believe in him? And how can they believe in him if*
> *they have never heard about him? And how can they*
> *hear about him unless someone tells them? And how*
> *will anyone go and tell them without being sent? That*
> *is why the Scriptures say, "How beautiful are the feet of*
> *messengers who bring good news!"* (Romans 10:14-15).

This I Believe
It is my joy and responsibility to share
the good news of Christ.

Stop Running

Y ou are so important to God. He has millions of children, but none is of more value than you. That's the greatness of God's infinite love and grace. It's the reason He continues to draw you into the circle of His love. You can keep running if you choose, but He's right here, waiting to receive you to Himself.

Luke 15 tells the story of the prodigal son. A young man asked his father for his inheritance early, and then left to live a life of his own choosing. He soon ran out of money and friends and decided to return home to work for his father—if his father would take him back. Verse 20 is one of those happy endings we women love: "And while he was still a long way off, his father saw him coming. Filled with love and compassion, he ran to his son, embraced him, and kissed him."

Jesus has come from the Father to show you the way back to life and truth. You may have trusted Christ at some point in your life and yet not be in close fellowship with Him now. You could be a prodigal. Does that shock you? Come back to Jesus today. Let the celebration begin!

> "This son of mine was dead and has now
> returned to life. He was lost, but now he is
> found." So the party began (Luke 15:24).

This I Believe
The loving heart of God is eager to restore anyone.

Walking in the Spirit

When was the last time you cried for those who don't know the Savior? That kind of compassion only comes from the Holy Spirit. A deep desire to reach others isn't something you "work up." No, it's a result of *walking in the power of the Holy Spirit.* It comes from having our minds and hearts *saturated* with the Word of God.

Ask the Lord to give you a burden for those around you today. And ask Him for opportunities to reach out with compassion and hope…right where you are.

*The seeds of good deeds become a tree of life; a
wise person wins friends* (Proverbs 11:30).

This I Believe
I will have an opportunity today to demonstrate
the tenderness of Jesus to someone.

A Flag Waves Tall

Fort McHenry. Do you recognize the name? If you're a student of history, you know that's where our star-spangled banner proudly flew through the night while "bombs were bursting in air." It stood tall in spite of being bombarded hundreds of times through the night. Our *flag* is a symbol of freedom.

Some people debate whether or not we live in a Christian nation. But what's really important is that our nation allows us to be Christians…and that means the freedom to give hope to those who are bombarded by the cruelties of life. Our banner—the Bible—stands tall. It's filled with promises of a better tomorrow. So when you celebrate our nation's independence and your own, thank God for the freedom you enjoy to worship Him and tell others about Him.

Godliness makes a nation great, but sin is a
disgrace to any people (Proverbs 14:34).

This I Believe
It is important to exercise my freedom and
support my local church.

Assurance of Heirs

One of the wonderful things about a relationship with Jesus Christ is knowing for sure where we'll spend eternity. The Bible says we can have that certainty. It's a little like marriage. If someone asks if you're married, you don't answer, "I think so." You proudly wear the evidence of your relationship—usually a ring. You also have a license signed by a pastor or judge and two witnesses.

The same thing about your citizenship. If you were born in the United States, there's no question about whether you're a citizen. You are. And the same thing is true when it comes to your relationship with God. The Bible puts it this way, "Since we are his children, we are his heirs. In fact, together with Christ we are heirs of God's glory" (Romans 8:17). Like marriage and citizenship, you *can* know for sure.

> *Because we are his children, God has sent the Spirit*
> *of his Son into our hearts, prompting us to call*
> *out, "Abba, Father." Now you are no longer a slave*
> *but God's own child. And since you are his child,*
> *God has made you his heir (Galatians 4:6-7).*

This I Believe
I can claim my spiritual inheritance every day.

A Word Carefully Spoken

Have you stood at graveside with a friend who has just buried his or her child? It's devastating. Words are never adequate in times like those. Only God's Word, carefully spoken and directed by the Holy Spirit, can even begin to help the grievers comprehend and experience God's love and grace. It's times like these that, with the Holy Spirit's leading, it's a joy to tell burdened people they are loved by the God of all comfort.

Ask God to help you be sensitive to the hurts of those around you...to be ready to comfort from God's Word and share the good news of a loving heavenly Father. God *will* use you for His glory.

> *We who are strong must be considerate of those who are sensitive about things like this. We must not just please ourselves. We should help others do what is right and build them up in the Lord* (Romans 15:1-2).

This I Believe
The Holy Spirit will lead me to someone who needs to be encouraged.

Don't Blame the Pudding

A desperate teenager whined, "But, Mom, it's the pudding's fault! I did everything like you said. I can't help it if *they* made it wrong." Her mother took one look at the mess and knew her daughter hadn't paid attention to her instructions. "Dear, if you don't stir it all the time while it's cooking, you get lumps. Didn't you hear me when I explained that?"

Her daughter answered, "No, Mom. I guess I was more worried about finding all the ingredients."

Isn't that just like us? We're so anxious to blame something or someone else for our own wrongdoing. Dear one, don't blame the pudding. The best thing you can do in your relationships with others, and especially with God, is to admit when you've done something wrong.

Confess your sins to each other and pray for each other so that you may be healed. The earnest prayer of a righteous person has great power and produces wonderful results (James 5:16).

This I Believe
Admitting when I am wrong is cleansing for my soul.

Change Your World

Mary Ann had a special burden for her neighbor, Eleanor. Eleanor's grandson, Dan, was involved with drugs and alcohol and couldn't keep a steady job. Mary Ann began faithfully praying for Dan, asking God to intervene in his life. It wasn't long before Dan decided to change his life. He stopped using drugs and alcohol and joined the navy.

Friend, what a privilege we have. God has chosen to let us help Him transform the world through our prayers. Pray for your neighbors and co-workers today. Pray they will come to know Christ in a personal way. Pray they will understand God's will for their lives. And also pray that their lives will please and honor God.

God wants to enlist you to change the world for eternity.

We have not stopped praying for you since we first heard about you. We ask God to give you complete knowledge of his will and to give you spiritual wisdom and understanding. Then the way you live will always honor and please the Lord, and your lives will produce every kind of good fruit. All the while, you will grow as you learn to know God better and better (Colossians 1:9-10).

This I Believe

The world will change one person at a time
as Christ rules individual hearts.

Enough

When trying circumstances come (and they will), never forget that "God will be all that you need...when all that you need is God." This reminds me of a story about a pastor. He called his local newspaper to give them the title of his Sunday sermon. He was planning to preach on the Twenty-third Psalm, so he told the reporter his message was "The Lord Is My Shepherd." Thinking there might be more, the reporter asked, "Is that all there is?" The minister smiled and answered, "That's enough!" And that's just how it appeared in the newspaper: "The Lord Is My Shepherd...and That's Enough!"

Choose to follow Him completely today.

The Lord is my shepherd; I have all that I need. He lets me rest in green meadows; he leads me beside peaceful streams. He renews my strength. He guides me along right paths, bringing honor to his name. Even when I walk through the darkest valley, I will not be afraid, for you are close beside me. Your rod and your staff protect and comfort me. You prepare a feast for me in the presence of my enemies. You honor me by anointing my head with oil. My cup overflows with blessings. Surely your goodness and unfailing love will pursue me all the days of my life, and I will live in the house of the Lord forever (Psalm 23).

This I Believe

I believe every word of this psalm.

Ever with the Lord

I love the verse of promise that says, "We will be with the Lord forever" (1 Thessalonians 4:17). No matter how difficult life might be, those words always bring deep encouragement. "We will be with the Lord forever." That statement is the capstone of our salvation. When we're weary, it will give us rest. When we're tired, it will spur us on. When we're discouraged, it will bring lasting hope.

If you've lost a loved one, take heart! You'll soon be joined eternally. If you're enduring physical pain, take heart! You're going to a land where there'll be no more suffering. If you're financially strapped, take heart! The streets of our eternal home are paved with gold.

Just a little longer, friend, and "we will be with the Lord forever."

The Lord himself will come down from heaven with a commanding shout, with the voice of the archangel, and with the trumpet call of God. First, the Christians who have died will rise from their graves. Then, together with them, we who are still alive and remain on the earth will be caught up in the clouds to meet the Lord in the air. Then we will be with the Lord forever. So encourage each other with these words (1 Thessalonians 4:16-18).

This I Believe
I know with confidence where
I will spend eternity.

God's Demands

God demands more of us than merely being religious. In fact, He insists on what a friend of mine calls "cross-bearing" faith. That may mean getting involved with those who are suffering—those with pains and problems. As Christian women, we have such an incredible privilege in bringing help and comfort. And this goes beyond our families. It extends to our neighbors, friends, and colleagues.

Service begins with the cross...the cross Jesus bore on our behalf. Dear one, there are people in your life who need your help. They may not even know Christ. Take a moment to "bear their cross" and express to them the love of Jesus Christ.

> *After washing their feet, [Jesus] put on his robe again*
> *and sat down and asked, "Do you understand what I*
> *was doing? You call me 'Teacher' and 'Lord,' and you*
> *are right, because that's what I am. And since I, your*
> *Lord and Teacher, have washed your feet, you ought*
> *to wash each other's feet. I have given you an example*
> *to follow. Do as I have done to you"* (John 13:12-15).

This I Believe
My hands and feet can be used by God to
minister to those in need—perhaps today.

Grubs and Goulash

A group of missionaries encountered a tribe that had little contact with the outside world. They made the tribal people feel more at ease by sharing meals with them. A special delicacy were fat, white grubs about an inch long and half an inch thick. Oh my!

Even the disciples likely ran across this dilemma. As He sent His men out on their first missionary trip, He said, "When you enter a town and are welcomed, eat what is set before you."

Here's the point. Honor your neighbors in their homes. It's a great way to open the door to talk about spiritual matters.

> [Jesus said,] "Whenever you enter someone's home, first say, 'May God's peace be on this house.' If those who live there are peaceful, the blessing will stand; if they are not, the blessing will return to you. Don't move around from home to home. Stay in one place, eating and drinking what they provide. Don't hesitate to accept hospitality, because those who work deserve their pay" (Luke 10:5-7).

This I Believe
When sharing the good news,
I will follow Jesus' teachings.

If the Barn
Needs Painting...

I'm sure you've heard the saying, "If the barn needs painting, paint it!" And it's so true. Do you know that as a child of God, you are to radiate God's beauty and glory? Think of it as God's paint. The Bible says, "A glad heart makes a happy face" (Proverbs 15:13). A shining face, radiant with the love and joy of Jesus Christ, is a witness to all you come into contact with. Your countenance often speaks much louder than words.

Never underestimate the power of a glowing face that comes from meeting with God. May your face and mine reveal time spent alone with God and in His Word.

The life of the godly is full of light and joy, but the light of the wicked will be snuffed out (Proverbs 13:9).

This I Believe
My outward countenance reflects
my inward condition.

Justice, Mercy, and Grace

Stuart Briscoe has a great illustration on "justice, mercy, and grace." His young son had been disobedient and needed to be punished. The wooden spoon was called for: ten "swats" in the appropriate place for discipline. That's justice. But Stuart stopped with only seven. His son was crying but asked why. His father explained that it was "mercy."

The boy was sent to his room to think about what had happened. Later, Stuart called up the stairs, "Son, how about going for ice cream? I'm buying." His son happily accepted the offer but wondered why the change in heart. Stuart explained: ten whacks were justice, stopping short was mercy, and ice cream—an undeserved gift—that's total grace.

And so too our loving heavenly Father proves we're His children through His justice, tempered with His mercy, and guided by His great grace.

How great is our Lord! His power is absolute! His understanding is beyond comprehension! (Psalm 147:5).

This I Believe

God's power is most evident through
His justice, mercy, and grace.

Not Me!

I've said it myself: "God, if You're depending on me to win souls for You, it won't happen. I'm just not up to the task." Well, here's a shocker: None of us will *ever* lead anyone to Christ. When a person receives Christ, it's *the work of the Holy Spirit.* That's why we can never boast…or be discouraged regarding our sharing the gospel of Christ. The responsibility for what Scripture calls "life-giving fruit" belongs to the Holy Spirit. *He* changes the lives of those who respond to our witness, not us.

Isn't that a freeing thought? The power of our Lord Jesus Christ is available to all who trust and obey Him. We're simply called to be faithful in proclaiming the great news. We are to leave the results to our heavenly Father.

> [Jesus] told them, "Go into all the world and preach
> the Good News to everyone. Anyone who believes and
> is baptized will be saved. But anyone who refuses
> to believe will be condemned" (Mark 16:15-16).

This I Believe
My requirement is to be obedient
and respond to God-given opportunities.

Precious Little Hands

Wendy and Dave faithfully pray for, care for, and share Christ with their neighbors. As a result, they are seeing spiritual changes within their neighborhood. They are also having a huge impact on their own children. One day their eight-year-old daughter, Karin, asked her young friend Anna an important question: "Anna, are you sure if you died today that you would go to heaven?"

Anna shook her head. She wasn't sure.

Karin continued. "Would you like to ask Jesus into your heart?"

Anna smiled and nodded.

Karin took Anna's hand and led her to Christ through prayer.

Oh dear friend, we can help win the world to Christ through our children. Pray for them and with them. Teach them about Christ. Live a godly life before them. The world's future is in their precious little hands.

O Lord, our Lord, your majestic name fills the earth!
Your glory is higher than the heavens. You have taught
children and infants to tell of your strength, silencing
your enemies and all who oppose you (Psalm 8:1-2).

This I Believe
The innocence of a child is a perfect
expression of Jesus' love.

Procrastination

I never seem to have enough time in my day to get everything done. Can you relate? So I procrastinate; I put everything off until tomorrow. No doubt one of Satan's greatest weapons of deceit is procrastination. "Tomorrow I'll witness to that neighbor." "Tomorrow I'll bake those cookies for the shelter." "As soon as I know more about the Bible, I'll begin sharing the good news of the gospel." Tomorrow!

God's Word says, "Today is the day of salvation" (2 Corinthians 6:2). *Now* is the time. In God's eyes, we are to redeem the time He's given us. We are to *take every opportunity* we can *to share our faith*.

Has God laid someone on your heart? Don't put off talking to that person. Life is short, so the time is now.

As God's partners, we beg you not to accept this marvelous gift of God's kindness and then ignore it. For God says, "At just the right time, I heard you. On the day of salvation, I helped you." Indeed, the "right time" is now. Today is the day of salvation (2 Corinthians 6:1-2).

This I Believe

I may only have this day to speak to someone about believing in Christ.

Send Out Workers

Mary invited her friend Chris to her home. She lived on a farm, and since the corn had been harvested, Mary's dad offered the girls a chance to earn some spending money. Their job was to glean the fields and pick up leftover ears. It was hard work, but the two girls had a good time.

Jesus also asked for workers. He chose disciples and sent them out into all the towns and places He planned to visit. And He sends us out too. The Lord of the spiritual harvest has done the real work for us. Sometimes the task of spreading the gospel can seem overwhelming. But all God asks us to do is start gleaning the fields, one ear at a time, right where we are.

[Jesus said,] "The harvest is great, but the workers are few. So pray to the Lord who is in charge of the harvest; ask him to send more workers into his fields" (Luke 10:2).

This I Believe

I may be privileged to glean a soul today where someone else has sown the seed.

Share Christ
with the World

As a college student, Karen went on a mission trip to Asia. When she returned, Karen had a burden to share Christ with international students on her campus. One day, Karen met a student from Korea named Wee. Karen shared her faith, using Campus Crusade for Christ's *Four Spiritual Laws* booklet. She carefully explained each page to her new friend.

When Karen finished, Wee chose to invite Jesus Christ into her life. As Karen prayed a sentence in English, Wee repeated it in Korean. Now Karen and Wee meet regularly for Bible study.

You don't have to travel the world to share Christ with the world! There are many international students in the United States who would love to hear about Christ.

[Jesus said,] "I have been given all authority in heaven and on earth. Therefore, go and make disciples of all the nations, baptizing them in the name of the Father and the Son and the Holy Spirit" (Matthew 28:18-19).

This I Believe
Language isn't a barrier
to my witnessing.

Stick Out Your Tongue

So often what's on the outside is an indicator of what's happening on the inside. Problems just don't hide. For instance, many gardeners can simply look at a leaf and know if the plant has a problem. Or remember when your mother would say, "Stick out your tongue"? Your tongue was a barometer of your health.

What you are on the *outside* often is evidence of your spiritual need on the *inside*. That's why we want to be refreshed and empowered by the work of the Holy Spirit every day. He helps us grow spiritually so that our insides will reflect on our outsides. He cleanses us from sin—from the disease of this world that can quickly drag us down.

While people look at *outward* appearances, God looks at our *hearts*:

> The LORD said to Samuel, "Don't judge by
> his appearance or height, for I have rejected
> him. The LORD doesn't see things the way you see
> them. People judge by outward appearance, but
> the LORD looks at the heart" (1 Samuel 16:7).

This I Believe
Only God can see the true condition
of my heart.

The Milkman's Best Delivery

As a child, Cheryl Prewitt was often in her father's small grocery store. Almost every day the milkman delivered to the store. When he saw Cheryl, he would say, "How's my little Miss America?"

At first she giggled. Then she became comfortable with the idea, and the words became a goal. In 1980, Cheryl stood on a stage in Atlantic City and was crowned Miss America!

My friend, the milkman probably never realized his greeting to Cheryl would become a reality. In the same way, you may not realize how you can influence people with your words. First Thessalonians 5:11 says: "Encourage each other and build each other up." Look around you. Be quick to praise and encourage someone. Offer to pray for them.

Be like the milkman and deliver words that nourish people's hearts.

> Be joyful. Grow to maturity. Encourage each other.
> Live in harmony and peace. Then the God of love
> and peace will be with you (2 Corinthians 13:11).

This I Believe
Every word of encouragement is an
investment in someone's life.

Wanted: Available Servants

Marjie received Christ at a high school youth retreat. When she got home, she told one of her neighbors, Nancy, about the retreat. Marjie quickly realized Nancy was interested in knowing Christ. She ran to her car and got a Campus Crusade *Four Spiritual Laws* booklet. She carefully went through each page with Nancy. Then Nancy invited Jesus Christ into her life through prayer. She couldn't wait to tell her husband when he got home!

And Marjie? Well, she was excited that God had used her, even though she was a new believer, to lead someone to Christ.

Friend, you don't have to be a theologian to share your faith. God is looking for available servants. Step out in faith and share Jesus Christ with someone. Just tell your story, and let God take care of the rest.

Jesus told him, "I entered this world to render judgment—to give sight to the blind and to show those who think they see that they are blind" (John 9:39).

This I Believe
The Holy Spirit will use my availability.

The Bottom Line

What's the bottom line?" "Show me the numbers!" We've been persuaded into believing success is only measured by statistics. Everyone wants big numbers, big results. But God evaluates success quite differently. He knows our mistakes, where we've missed the mark, our sins, and He still forgives us.

The Bible says while man looks on the outside, God looks at the *heart*. The Lord simply asks us to be faithful and obedient. And it all starts with a personal relationship with Jesus Christ.

You don't have to worry about showing God "the data." Through His Son, Jesus Christ, He'll call you a success right where you are.

> [Jesus said,] "If any of you wants to be my follower, you must turn from your selfish ways, take up your cross, and follow me. If you try to hang on to your life, you will lose it. But if you give up your life for my sake, you will save it. And what do you benefit if you gain the whole world but lose your own soul? Is anything worth more than your soul?" (Matthew 16:24-26).

This I Believe
My success will be measured in eternity.

Whoa to You

Young Jenny was wiggling in her seat on the way home from church. Her parents were discussing the morning's sermon. The pastor had been preaching from Luke 10 about repentance. He had emphasized the phrase "Woe to you" for those who had not repented.

Jenny's parents asked her if she knew the meaning of "woe." Jenny loved horses, so she thought it was "whoa," which meant the command "Stop!"

Her parents chuckled for a moment and then explained "woe" meant "distress or sorrow." Suddenly the parents realized that repentance is a 180-degree turn. In order to go in the opposite direction, you first have to stop. That's so true.

Friend, if you're heading in the wrong direction, pull back on the reins of your life, stop, and turn around. Let God change the direction of your future.

> Peter replied, "Each of you must repent of your sins, turn to God, and be baptized in the name of Jesus Christ to show that you have received forgiveness for your sins. Then you will receive the gift of the Holy Spirit" (Acts 2:38).

This I Believe
I will stop today and see if God
has a new direction for me.

Why Witness?

Quite frankly, I would never tell another person about Christ if I waited until I felt like it. But Jesus said, "Come, follow me, and I will show you how to fish for people!" We tell others about God because of the wonderful model we have in Jesus Christ—and because He commands us to tell others about Him. It's as simple as that.

My husband, Bill, was one of the most fervent soul winners I've known. Living with him for those many years was quite an education. He so often ended his messages with "Tell everyone who will listen about Christ."

So here's a tip on telling others about Jesus Christ: Don't wait for your emotions to give you permission—that may never happen. Instead, be obedient. Be a witness of His love and grace.

Since we have been made right in God's sight by faith, we have peace with God because of what Jesus Christ our Lord has done for us. Because of our faith, Christ has brought us into this place of undeserved privilege where we now stand, and we confidently and joyfully look forward to sharing God's glory (Romans 5:1-2).

This I Believe
It doesn't matter how I feel about
sharing my faith. It is a command.

Witnessing
That Can't Fail

Sometimes it's hard to know what other people need. But here's one thing I'm confident of: Your neighbor needs a word of encouragement. She could be a mom who's almost at the end of her rope or a friend who's husband just lost his job.

Ask the Lord to give you the right words to say. I can't tell you how many times I've been sharing my faith with someone while frantically asking God to give me just the right words. And He put in my mouth the very words that needed to be said.

Success in witnessing is simply taking the opportunity to share Christ in the power of the Holy Spirit. The results are up to God. When we obey Him and are motivated by love, we can't fail!

The Kingdom of God is not a matter of what we eat or drink, but of living a life of goodness and peace and joy in the Holy Spirit. If you serve Christ with this attitude, you will please God, and others will approve of you, too (Romans 14:17-18).

This I Believe
If I knew I could not fail,
who would I share my faith with today?
I'll do it!

Addicted to Credit

There are so many diseases that plague our world. Medical researchers work feverishly to discover cures for them. But there's one epidemic that doesn't have medical researchers working for a cure. It's threatening our families and homes as never before. The disease is debt. Economists tell us that the general population owes far too much money. Many families are in debt way beyond their income levels.

The real cause of most debt is general discontentment, and we are warned about that in God's Word. Jesus taught that satisfaction does not come from "things," yet we ignore His warning. As Christians, we are called to love people not things.

Spend your energy on people, and possessions will find their proper place.

Seek the Kingdom of God above all else,
and live righteously, and he will give you
everything you need (Matthew 6:33).

This I Believe
I will value people more than possessions.

Country Doctor

Despite all our differences, such as age, background, financial status, the Bible says people *all* have one thing in common. God declares we are all sinners. Billy Graham tells the story of a country doctor who was unable to diagnose one of his patients' illness. Finally the doctor asked, "Have you ever had this problem before?"

The man quickly said, "Oh, yes, doctor, many times."

The doctor happily explained, "Well then, you have it again!"

The fact is, as long as we're in this life, there's no way we can avoid the problem of sin. It infects all of us. We have it again and again. Thankfully, the Bible provides a wonderful prescription: "If we confess our sins to [Jesus Christ], he is faithful and just to forgive us our sins and to cleanse us from all wickedness" (1 John 1:9). That's a life-saving remedy.

[Jesus] gave his life to free us from every kind of sin, to cleanse us, and to make us his very own people, totally committed to doing good deeds (Titus 2:14).

This I Believe
Every day my sins need to be forgiven.

Seize the Moment

Have you talked with anyone about Jesus Christ during the past week? During the past month? In the past year? Since you became a Christian? Now, I'm not asking just to lay a guilt trip on you. In fact, I'm sure you're not alone if you haven't witnessed as much as you'd like. But you know what? When you fail to share your faith, you miss out on one of God's greatest blessings.

I can't tell you the number of times on an airplane, in a department store, or with one of my children that God used the moment and gave me just the right words to share Jesus and His wisdom. Today, take advantage of one of the opportunities God will give you. You'll experience incredible joy in sharing Christ.

In fact, it may begin with a very simple comment and lead to a full-blown conversation about God's love and salvation through Jesus.

The Good News about the Kingdom will be preached throughout the whole world, so that all nations will hear it; and then the end will come (Matthew 24:14).

This I Believe
Since I do not know the moment of
Christ's return, I will
seize every moment to share God's love.

Dark Nights and Difficult Days

Whatever you're facing today, your heavenly Father knows all about it. We can't rid our lives of those dark nights and difficult days. Even Jesus Christ experienced them while He was on earth. You may be afraid or doubtful at times, but you can be sure God loves you. That will never change. Not even when the storms of life are beating all around you. If your faith is in Christ, it may be shaken, but it will never be destroyed.

Claim this promise right where you are, in *whatever* circumstance you find yourself. And recognize God is using your situation to mature you, to prepare you to be a more effective servant for His kingdom.

Don't be afraid, little flock. For it gives your Father
great happiness to give you the Kingdom (Luke 12:32).

This I Believe
In times of distress I will remember that
God keeps His promises.

Enduring Friend

At a conference, Bill introduced me as his "beloved, beautiful, charming, adorable, loving wife." He also called me the super-wife, the super-mom, and the super-grandma. Bill and I definitely had times of disagreement in our marriage, but our bond stayed strong because we were willing to sacrifice ourselves for each other.

Dear one, are you having problems in your marriage? Practice patience. Be slow to anger, quick to forgive, and abounding in love. *Humbly* sacrifice yourself as Jesus did for us. With love, determine to work together with one heart and one purpose.

Try this today: Instead of hurling insults during an argument, build up your spouse by loving him through your words and deeds. You may soon find *him* referring to *you* as his beloved, beautiful, charming, adorable, loving wife.

Always be humble and gentle. Be patient with
each other, making allowance for each other's
faults because of your love. Make every effort
to keep yourselves united in the Spirit, binding
yourselves together with peace (Ephesians 4:2-3).

This I Believe
When a husband and wife love Christ, His Spirit
binds them beyond circumstances.

Fixing X-rays

You may have heard about the doctor who found a life-threatening malignant spot on an X-ray. The doctor told his patient he had two choices: go through extensive surgery or touch up the X-ray to hide the problem.

Yes, I know this wouldn't really happen in real life. But friend, believe it or not, we try doing this for our spiritual condition. Covering up our sinful hearts does no good. It doesn't solve the real problem. Medical help is required! The good news is that Jesus Christ provided the cure. He's taken care of that sinful condition you face and provided the healing balm of eternal life with God.

Today, spiritually speaking, you have a clean bill of health for eternity.

Have mercy on me, O God, because of your unfailing love. Because of your great compassion, blot out the stain of my sins. Wash me clean from my guilt (Psalm 51:1-2).

This I Believe
My spiritual well-being is dependent on a
daily commitment to God's truth.

Frank's Most at the Last

Frank Lynn was 43 when he was diagnosed with an incurable form of cancer. Within days, he gave his life to Jesus—something his wife and sons had prayed for often for many years. His cold, stoic heart melted. Formal handshakes became bear hugs with his sons. He became the listening, loving husband every wife wants.

Three weeks before Frank died, the boys wrote their dad a letter of love and read it to him. It was a time of weeping and closure. Frank and his family came to the end with no regrets.

Unfortunately, many of us won't have that chance. Dear one, don't wait to tell your parents, your spouse, or your children how much they mean to you. You can't take back yesterday, and we aren't guaranteed tomorrow. Make the most of today.

When people work, their wages are not a gift, but something they have earned. But people are counted as righteous, not because of their work, but because of their faith in God who forgives sinners (Romans 4:4-5).

This I Believe
I want to capture the joy in every day.

God's Peace

In January of 1960, two men went where no man had ever gone before...or since. They plunged into the deepest spot in the ocean at the Marianas Trench, nearly seven miles down. That's a full mile deeper than Mount Everest is tall. At that depth, the pressure is tremendous—more than 200 million pounds. And yet they found life as tranquil as can be. No matter the storms that raged on the surface, the ocean below was calm and peaceful.

This is the way our Christian lives should be. No matter what storms rage around us, deep down we have peace. Under the greatest pressure, God gives us calm assurance to face every day.

> [Jesus said,] "I am leaving you with a gift—peace of mind and heart. And the peace I give is a gift the world cannot give. So don't be troubled or afraid" (John 14:27).

This I Believe
The peace of God is beyond understanding.
I choose to live in His peace.

Grace over Temptation

Some days it seems I fall into every trap at Satan's disposal. I'm tempted to gossip. I react unkindly to people who hurt those I love. I feel jealous. I lack a healthy sense of self-worth because of criticism I didn't earn.

The temptations that plague us are numberless. The Scriptures tell us so. But be encouraged! You and I not only have Christ's sympathy, we also have His concern. And we have His promise that the Father will grant us grace to withstand temptation. God's forgiving grace never ends.

Prayerfully place each one of those temptations that hound you under the control of God's Spirit. And don't be afraid. The God who redeemed you will also keep you...forever. Nothing can take you from His loving hands.

Let all who take refuge in you [O God] rejoice; let them sing joyful praises forever. Spread your protection over them, that all who love your name may be filled with joy. For you bless the godly, O LORD; you surround them with your shield of love (Psalm 5:11-12).

This I Believe
No temptation can overtake me
as I walk in His love.

Journey for Jill

Sue and Paula are running partners. Every Sunday they attend church together, and then they go for a six-mile run. One Sunday they noticed another friend was in pain during church. They discovered Jill was unable to work and needed a kidney transplant. Sue and Paula wanted to help with Jill's medical expenses so they decided to organize a run/walk event to raise money. Church members quickly joined in to help. Another local church donated $2000. Almost the entire town got involved. On race day, 140 people competed. The event raised $10,500!

Jill received a transplant, and she is so grateful that Sue and Paula put their love into action.

Oh friend, Jesus said to love one another. This will prove we are His disciples. So lace up your shoes and help someone today.

Share each other's burdens, and in this way obey the law of Christ. If you think you are too important to help someone, you are only fooling yourself. You are not that important (Galatians 6:2-3).

This I Believe
I show God's love
by helping people.

Keep Praying

Cindy prayer-walked a neighborhood near her church every day. After a year, she wondered if she was making a difference. One Friday, while her eyes were fixed on a particular house, she prayed, "Lord, is this doing any good?" She continued her prayer-walk. Two days later, when Cindy attended church, she met a new couple whose names were Todd and Amanda. They had never been to church before.

They shared they'd been divorced, remarried, and separated several times. Two days earlier, they had decided they needed God's help. It was during the same hour that Cindy was prayer-walking! And the house where Cindy had stopped and prayed was Todd and Amanda's.

Dear friend, "devote yourselves to prayer with an alert mind and a thankful heart" (Colossians 4:2). When you're tired of praying for something or someone, remember: *In God's perfect time, He will answer.* Keep praying!

Live wisely among those who are not believers, and make the most of every opportunity. Let your conversation be gracious and attractive so that you will have the right response for everyone (Colossians 4:5-6).

This I Believe
My prayers can change someone's life.

Labor Day

When he was a young boy, Harry Ironside worked weekends to help his widowed mother make ends meet. His boss, a Scottish shoemaker, taught Harry the *real* story of a man's "soul." One day young Harry questioned the shoemaker as to why he made the shoes so durable. After all, if they wore out quickly, wouldn't customers come back sooner?

The shoemaker said, "Harry, I don't cobble shoes for the money. I do it for the glory of God."

Harry learned at the hand of this godly cobbler that, as it says in the Bible, we are to "work willingly at whatever [we] do, as though [we] were working for the Lord rather than for people" (Colossians 3:23). My challenge for you is to do all you do to the glory of Jesus Christ.

Whatever you do or say, do it as a representative
of the Lord Jesus, giving thanks through him
to God the Father (Colossians 3:17).

This I Believe
Everything I do is significant because
I do it for God's glory.

Look to God

Two years ago a doctor walked into the room where I was waiting. He looked at me and said, "Mrs. Bright, your husband is a very ill man." His diagnosis of pulmonary fibrosis was not what I expected, but I know God was not surprised.

Since that day, God has used many passages of Scripture to minister to me. One of the most recent is Psalm 57, where David writes of God's faithfulness in times of trouble. One of the key verses says: "My heart is confident in you, O God; no wonder I can sing your praises" (verse 7).

Oh dear friend, I can rejoice in the midst of trials. Why? Because my trust is in God's unfailing love and faithfulness. So whatever you're going through today, look to God. Rejoice in His goodness. He will encourage your heart because He loves you.

Have mercy on me, O God, have mercy! I look to you for protection. I will hide beneath the shadow of your wings until the danger passes by. I cry out to God Most High, to God who will fulfill his purpose for me (Psalm 57:1-2).

This I Believe
The love of God will give me the
strength I need for each day.

Love Is Action

Marla prayed for a particular family in her neighborhood. She visited them and expressed her love and care for them. One day the mother shared her concern regarding her daughter's rebelliousness. So Marla prayed for Christina. She invited Christina to attend a youth retreat with her church. That weekend Christina received Jesus Christ into her heart! Now their entire family is active in church. They also meet with Marla once a month to pray for their neighbors.

Dear friend, Jesus tells us to love our neighbors. Love is an *action* word. Pray for your neighbors. Take every opportunity to get to know them. Ask God to show you ways to care for them and help meet their needs.

Jesus replied, "What does the law of
Moses say? How do you read it?"

The man answered, "You must love the LORD your God
with all your heart, all your soul, all your strength, and
all your mind." And, "Love your neighbor as yourself."

"Right!" Jesus told him. "Do this and
you will live!" (Luke 10:26-28).

This I Believe
I really *can* make a difference in
the lives of the people near me.

Out of Control

Several young boys were playing on a large bulldozer, pretending to operate the massive machine. Unfortunately, the operator had left the key in the ignition, and the engine roared to life when they turned it. When the steel monster moved, the frightened boys quickly jumped off. Before the dozer could be stopped, a dozen cars were totaled and several houses and telephone poles were damaged. Even some fire hydrants were sheared off.

Oh how that parallels life! Machines work best when under the control of a *qualified* operator. Our lives work best when we place ourselves in the hands of our Operator—God! He steers us down the road to peace and tranquility rather than damage and destruction.

When you turn control *completely* over to the One who created you, your heart experiences freedom and your life is more useful. Why not try it today?

> *O LORD, I have come to you for protection; don't let me be disgraced. Save me and rescue me, for you do what is right. Turn your ear to listen to me, and set me free. Be my rock of safety where I can always hide. Give the order to save me, for you are my rock and my fortress* (Psalm 71:1-3).

This I Believe
I surrender everything to my
Lord and Savior, Jesus Christ.

Persistence Pays Off

Success comes from taking just *one more step* beyond where you feel like giving up. Such was the case with Madame Curie and her husband, Pierre. They discovered radium, but not without endless hours of searching, disappointing failures, and discouraging comments from those who said it couldn't be done. Late one night, the Curies decided to go back to their humble laboratory. As they opened the door, they saw the eerie glow of a beautiful bluish light. Persistence had paid off. Radium was at last a reality.

When Jesus told His disciples to cast their nets *one more time,* it was in the very same place they had already cast them. But they obeyed and reaped a tremendous haul of fish!

Dear one, press on! Don't give up. All the battles fought… all the trials suffered…will seem like nothing when you meet your Savior face-to-face.

[Jesus] called out, "Fellows, have you caught any fish?"

"No," they replied.

Then he said, "Throw out your net on the right-hand side of the boat, and you'll get some!"

So they did, and they couldn't haul in the net because there were so many fish in it (John 21:4-6).

This I Believe
I will try and try again to accomplish
what God wants me to do.

Practice Makes Perfect

Paderewski was arguably one of the world's finest pianists. But he was the first to admit his ability didn't come by chance. His secret was constant practice. As a boy, he rehearsed for endless hours while other children played. As an adult, Paderewski was invited to give a command performance before the queen of England. After the concert, she said, "Mr. Paderewski, you are a true genius!" Humbly he responded, "Ah, your majesty…long before I was a 'genius,' I was a 'drudge.'"

Do you ever feel like a drudge? As the old saying goes, "The trouble with life is that it's so daily." Dear one, the Lord commands us to keep on. Stay faithful.

O LORD God of Heaven's Armies! Where is
there anyone as mighty as you, O LORD? You
are entirely faithful (Psalm 89:8).

This I Believe
I can trust God to honor my faithfulness.

Pray Blessings

Kelly is a lighthouse in her countryside neighborhood. Since it's difficult to prayer-walk the dirt roads, Kelly decided to prayer-drive. She got a box of door hangers and made a list of every home. Kelly drove to each house and stopped at the mailbox. As she was praying, she hung the door hanger on the side of the mailbox. On each hanger she had written her name and that she was praying for that family. If Kelly observed something about them, she would note it on her prayer list. As Kelly prayed, something unexpected happened. God began to give her a sincere love and concern for each neighbor.

Dear friend, when you pray for others, you will receive a supernatural love for them. Pray blessings on your neighbors today. You will be blessed in return.

The earth is the LORD's, and everything in it. The world and all its people belong to him. For he laid the earth's foundation on the seas and built it on the ocean depths (Psalm 24:1-2).

This I Believe
My neighborhood will be blessed by
my faithfulness to pray for them.

Quote and Float

Nancy went swimming at the local YMCA. As she swam laps, she quoted Bible verses out loud. A married couple, Dave and Irene, was swimming nearby. Irene was a Christian, but Dave was not.

Nancy's actions soon caught Dave's attention. He asked, "What are you doing?"

Nancy replied, "I'm working on my Bible memory verses."

Then Nancy shared the gospel with Dave. She quoted Scripture verses so he could clearly understand what she was teaching him.

As whistles blew and the swim team practiced nearby, Dave invited Christ into his life through prayer. He said, "I never knew. I've been religious all my life, but nobody ever explained to me that I could have a personal relationship with Jesus Christ."

Friend, keep God's Word hidden in your heart and mind. You never know when you will have the opportunity to share it.

Now, son of man, I [the Lord] am making you a watchman for the people of Israel. Therefore, listen to what I say and warn them for me (Ezekiel 33:7).

This I Believe
God's Word will always bring conviction to both the believer and the nonbeliever.

Your Rescue Mission

The *Titanic* was thought to be an unsinkable ship, but on April 14, 1912, it hit an iceberg and sank. More than 2200 people were aboard that ship; only 705 survived. However, most of the lifeboats were only half full. Many people were floating in the frigid waters. They cried for help, but the people in the lifeboats rowed away. Those who were already saved wouldn't go back for those who were dying. Hundreds of people froze to death.

Oh dear one, there are people everywhere who are sinking into a tragic eternity. Proverbs 24:11 says: "Rescue those who are unjustly sentenced to die; save them as they stagger to their death." Don't just sit in your lifeboat! Share the good news of Jesus Christ with someone today. Consider it your rescue mission.

> *Rescue those who are unjustly sentenced to die...Don't excuse yourself by saying, "Look, we didn't know." For God understands all hearts, and he sees you. He who guards your soul knows you knew. He will repay all people as their actions deserve* (Proverbs 24:11-12).

This I Believe
I have a responsibility to rescue those who are spiritually perishing.

Resurrection Power

Whacen a man leaves his wife and moves in with another woman, most of us would not give much hope for the marriage to survive. When Mario moved out, Michelle gave up on her marriage. But Mario wasn't happy with his choice for long. He was so desperate he considered suicide.

A dear friend encouraged Michelle not to give up and to pray for Mario. This friend put her faith into action. She contacted Mario and told him she and Michelle were praying for him. Six months later Mario received Jesus as his Savior. After lots of prayer and forgiveness, Mario and Michelle's marriage was restored.

Never underestimate the power of God. Never lose hope. His power is available to you no matter what your circumstances are. Talk with Him today.

I want to know Christ and experience the mighty power that raised him from the dead. I want to suffer with him, sharing in his death, so that one way or another I will experience the resurrection from the dead! (Philippians 3:10-11).

This I Believe
The power of prayer can work behind
the scenes to transform a life.

Ring Around the Collar

Remember the old television commercial where a poor homemaker was taunted with "ring around the collar"? She couldn't get the stains out of her husband's shirts. We know that is not impossible to do, and now we have so many products to help. But there is a stain that *is* impossible for us to remove. It's the stain that sin leaves on our lives. Unfortunately, like a soiled shirt, it is the normal everyday activities of life that dirties us with sin. Thank goodness cleaning up is possible through Christ. He paid the ultimate price to lift our stains. Rejoice in this verse: "By [God's] grace you have been saved" (Ephesians 2:5 NKJV).

Dear one, don't spend time trying to clean up. Go to Christ for forgiveness. He will make you clean and whole. If you've never had Jesus Christ clean that stain in your life, ask Him to be your Lord and Savior, and He will wash your sins away.

God saved you by his grace when you believed. And you can't take credit for this; it is a gift from God. Salvation is not a reward for the good things we have done, so none of us can boast about it (Ephesians 2:8-9).

This I Believe
God alone can cleanse my sins.

Spiritual Growth

admire beautiful Japanese bonsai trees. Gardeners fashion these amazing trees by tying off the taproots of the plants when they're very young. The result is that the tree is really undernourished. It's prevented from attaining its potential height. While the tree looks impressive in a pot, it's a different story when it comes to our Christian lives. When we cut ourselves off from the life-giving truth of the Holy Spirit, we are limited to being spiritual dwarves.

Dear one, commit yourself wholly to God. Enjoy the Father's everlasting, life-giving flow of divine grace. Don't deny yourself the privilege and opportunity of growing to full stature in Christ. The apostle Peter encourages us to "grow in grace and knowledge of our Lord and Savior Jesus Christ" (2 Peter 3:18).

Dear brothers and sisters, when troubles come your way, consider it an opportunity for great joy. For you know that when your faith is tested, your endurance has a chance to grow. So let it grow, for when your endurance is fully developed, you will be perfect and complete, needing nothing (James 1:2-4).

This I Believe
My spiritual growth may require some
pruning in my life.

The Best Conversation

What occupies your conversations lately? Politics? Relationships? The latest gossip? Why do we "clam up" when it comes to talking about the *best* news that ever happened? Dear one, we serve a living Savior who died on the cross for our sins. He rose from the dead. And through Him we receive the incredible gift of eternal life. People *want* to hear good news. Let the Bible do the talking for you. A verse as simple as John 3:16 will have a powerful effect: "For God loved the world so much that he gave his one and only Son, so that everyone who believes in him will not perish but have eternal life."

When was the last time you heard anything that positive on the evening news? Think today about the goodness of God and share His goodness with those around you.

*Fix your thoughts on what is true, and honorable,
and right, and pure, and lovely, and admirable.
Think about things that are excellent and worthy
of praise. Keep putting into practice all you learned
and received from me—everything you heard
from me and saw me doing. Then the God of
peace will be with you* (Philippians 4:8-9).

This I Believe
The good news of the gospel is the
only hope in a world of bad news.

Training Weight

Golf is a popular sport. Frequently players talk about their "handicap." It's an artificial disadvantage imposed on a player to equalize chances of winning. To an Olympic runner, a handicap is a weight added just for training purposes. It makes the runner work harder, preparing him for the actual race when he will run unencumbered. And in this race called "Life," the Bible urges us to lay aside every weight, every "handicap" that keeps us from being effective in our Christian walk and service.

Handicaps are helpful in training, but now the real race is on. Put aside those things that are slowing you down in your spiritual growth. Finish in such a way that you'll hear the Lord's affirmation, "Well done, good and faithful servant."

Since we are surrounded by such a huge crowd of witnesses to the life of faith, let us strip off every weight that slows us down, especially the sin that so easily trips us up. And let us run with endurance the race God has set before us (Hebrews 12:1).

This I Believe
Because God is faithful
to keep His promises,
I know I can endure.

Who Packs Your "Chute"?

Charles Plumb was a navy jet pilot during the Vietnam War. After 75 missions, his plane was hit by a missile. He ejected and parachuted into the hands of the enemy. He spent six years in a prison camp.

Years later, a man came to Plumb and said, "I'm the one who packed your parachute." Plumb realized how he had taken for granted the critical work of a fellow sailor he had never met.

We all have people who pack our parachutes—people we depend on. As believers, it's important that we primarily depend on the One who packs our "spiritual parachute"— Jesus Christ.

Every morning, begin your day depending on Him. Make the choice to rely on His faithful support and strength.

Give thanks to the LORD and proclaim his greatness. Let the whole world know what he has done. Sing to him; yes, sing his praises. Tell everyone about his wonderful deeds (Psalm 105:1-2).

This I Believe
When I begin each day thanking Jesus, I realize my dependence on Him.

Waiting to Hear

It was early Saturday afternoon. Becky and other church members had just distributed *Jesus* films to their community. Becky received a call from a woman named Ina. She'd just received a video and wanted to know more. Becky was tired, but she went to visit Ina. When Becky arrived, Ina's entire family was eagerly waiting on the front porch of their small home.

Becky explained the gospel, and then everyone stood up and held hands. She led them in prayer as they asked Jesus Christ into their hearts.

Friend, many people are waiting to hear about God's love. Share with someone this week.

If a man has a hundred sheep and one of them gets lost, what will he do? Won't he leave the ninety-nine others in the wilderness and go to search for the one that is lost until he finds it? And when he has found it, he will joyfully carry it home on his shoulders. When he arrives, he will call together his friends and neighbors, saying, "Rejoice with me because I have found my lost sheep." In the same way, there is more joy in heaven over one lost sinner who repents and returns to God than over ninety-nine others who are righteous and haven't strayed away! (Luke 15:4-7).

This I Believe
I can contribute to the joy in heaven
by telling someone about Jesus.

Your Worship

Liz was an avid painter during her high school and college years. When she entered the workforce, she dropped her paintbrush and palette to pursue a career. She was happy, but something seemed to be missing. When Liz took a mission trip to Italy, she was surrounded by some of the greatest artwork in history. Something stirred in her heart. She realized that the Lord created her to worship Him through her creativity. When she returned to the states, Liz came "back to the heart of her worship." She dusted off her art supplies and got to work.

Friend, what unique gifts and talents have you received from the Lord? Art? Singing? Dancing? Cooking? Writing? Encouraging? Find your special way to worship Him and get started.

In his grace, God has given us different gifts for doing certain things well. So if God has given you the ability to prophesy, speak out with as much faith as God has given you. If your gift is serving others, serve them well. If you are a teacher, teach well. If your gift is to encourage others, be encouraging. If it is giving, give generously. If God has given you leadership ability, take the responsibility seriously. And if you have a gift for showing kindness to others, do it gladly (Romans 12:6-8).

This I Believe
I will encourage people today
to pursue their passion.

Love

Have you had the experience of witnessing to a friend or a neighbor and asking God to help you? And He put the words in your mouth that you needed to say? Why are we so surprised! We have a faithful God.

That friend of yours who needs a word of encouragement—ask the Lord to give you the right words to say to her. That gal you have coffee with at the office? Trust God for His message to her through you.

As we come before the Lord with clean and pure hearts, He hears our prayers and is quick to answer them. Trust God to give you the words that need to be said to encourage the people you need to touch today. And remember, God is faithful!

If I could speak all the languages of earth and of angels, but didn't love others, I would only be a noisy gong or a clanging cymbal (1 Corinthians 13:1).

This I Believe
Words are the tools God uses
to reach our hearts
with the good news of His Son.

God Is in Control

What's your greatest need right now? If you are a mom at home, it might be patience. If you are a professional, it might be wisdom or strength or even courage. No matter now long or hard you think, you will not be able to come up with a circumstance beyond God's control. I hope this is great news for you today.

So much of the life you and I live as believers in Christ depends on our belief. Do you trust God to do what He says He will do? It's so simple. If we believe God will do what He says, the Bible tells us the blessing will be ours in every area of our lives. So go ahead. Place your trust in God and expect a great blessing from Him today.

He will keep you strong to the end so that you will be free from all blame on the day when our Lord Jesus Christ returns. God will do this, for he is faithful to do what he says, and he has invited you into partnership with his Son, Jesus Christ our Lord (1 Corinthians 1:8-9).

This I Believe
God is aware of my circumstances.
I trust Him completely.

Breath of God

My husband had to use oxygen the last months of his life. Without this "breath of life," Bill's lungs couldn't get what they needed from the air. We were so careful to make sure he always had a full oxygen tank.

As oxygen is important to our physical lives, the Spirit of God is important to our spiritual well-being. Without God's Spirit our faith grows weak. Here these words from a hymn by Edwin Hatch. Pray it with me, friend:

> Breathe on me, breath of God,
> until my heart is pure,
> until with Thee I will one be,
> to do and to endure.

In the strong name of Jesus Christ, we pray. Amen.

As [Jesus] spoke, he showed them the wounds in his hands and his side. They were filled with joy when they saw the Lord! Again he said, "Peace be with you. As the Father has sent me, so I am sending you." Then he breathed on them and said, "Receive the Holy Spirit" (John 20:20-22).

This I Believe
My life is sustained by the presence
of the Holy Spirit.

Christ's Coming

Sir Ernest Shackleton was an explorer of the Antarctic. On one trip, he found it necessary to temporarily leave some of his men behind. He promised he'd return for them as soon as the weather lifted. He didn't return the rest of that day…or the next or the one after that. Several weeks went by. Finally the day came when he did return. All the men were on the shoreline ready for rescue.

Why were they ready? One sailor said, "Every morning, Captain Wild, second in command, would tell us, 'Roll up your sea bags, boys…the boss may come back today!'"

And that is *our* charge from Jesus Christ! This could very well be the day He returns.

> *So you have sorrow now, but I will see you*
> *again; then you will rejoice, and no one*
> *can rob you of that joy* (John 16:22).

This I Believe
I will live today aware that Christ
could return any day.

Definition of Christianity

Christianity at its core is a personal relationship with Jesus. Take a moment to think about how you show these evidences of Christianity:

- In the home, it's thoughtfulness and kindness.
- In business, it's honesty and integrity.
- In play, it's fairness and genuine sportsmanship.
- Toward the fortunate, Christianity is congratulations.
- Toward the unfortunate, it is compassion.
- Toward the weak, it is helpfulness and encouragement.
- Toward temptations, it's Spirit-filled resistance.
- Toward the fallen, it's forgiveness.
- Toward pride, it's humility.
- And toward God, it's reverence, love, and obedience.

Beware of false prophets who come disguised as harmless sheep but are really vicious wolves. You can identify them by their fruit, that is, by the way they act...A good tree produces good fruit, and a bad tree produces bad fruit (Matthew 7:15-17).

This I Believe
Today I will make sure my
Christian walk matches my talk.

Drive-by Praying

Often the term "drive-by" has a negative connotation. But have you ever heard of drive-by praying? Well, 72-year-old Charlotte and 65-year-old Martha have. Both ladies decided to pray for the gang- and drug-infested neighborhoods in their city. Every week at midnight, Charlotte and Martha would drive to these areas. They sat in their car and prayed. People wondered what they were doing. If anyone asked, the ladies would answer, "We're praying for God's blessing for you."

Charlotte and Martha regularly prayed for one particular gang member named JJ. It wasn't long before he gave his life to Christ! Now he goes back to the same neighborhoods to share God's love.

Friend, serving God is never limited to young people. The "young at heart" can produce great spiritual fruit.

> *The godly will flourish like palm trees and grow strong like the cedars of Lebanon. For they are transplanted to the LORD's own house. They flourish in the courts of our God. Even in old age they will still produce fruit, they will remain vital and green* (Psalm 92:12-14).

This I Believe
Age isn't a negative in my service to God.

Hand Them the Keys

While most people try to stay out of jail, Dorothy visits one every week to minister to some of the prisoners. One day, she met an inmate who said, "I know you want to talk about Jesus. Well, it's not going to do any good because I'm a witch." The inmate went on to say she had done a lot of bad things. She'd joined a witches' coven because she thought Jesus wouldn't accept her.

Dorothy shared God's love and unconditional forgiveness. After a week of meeting, the inmate said yes to Jesus Christ!

Dear friend, there are many people who are imprisoned by their past mistakes. Share Christ with someone this week. When you do, you are handing her the keys to everlasting freedom.

Then the King will say to those on his right, "Come, you who are blessed by my Father, inherit the Kingdom prepared for you from the creation of the world" (Matthew 25:34).

This I Believe
I hold the keys to unlock someone
from her spiritual prison.

God's Heavenly Choir

Marjorie works on Long Island in New York City. Fortunately, her company was not close to the World Trade Center. Still, she and her co-workers mourned the nation's tragedy after the terrorist attacks on September 11, 2001.

When President Bush declared September 14 a national day of prayer, Marjorie asked for and received permission to lead the employees in a prayer service. She was also allowed to speak about Jesus Christ. As a result, God's love invaded her place of employment. As she shared the gospel with more than 100 employees, all of them audibly prayed to accept God.

Dear one, God has prepared hearts everywhere to receive His love. Pray for boldness, and then share His love with someone today. You may help another person become part of God's heavenly choir.

Sing about the glory of his name! Tell the world how glorious he is. Say to God, "How awesome are your deeds!" (Psalm 66:2-3).

This I Believe
My life may be the music that might
draw someone to Christ.

He Is Faithful

Karen had wanted to be a nurse since she was a child. However, a painful divorce left her with broken dreams. Now she had three young boys to support. She decided to trust God, and she applied for nursing school.

One morning as she was leaving the house, the phone rang. Karen had been accepted to nursing school! Suddenly she felt God's peace surround her. For the next year, she lived on a meager income, but God blessed her efforts. People from her church reached out to help Karen. Sometimes she would come home to find groceries on her doorstep. When Karen graduated, her nursing degree was a testimony of God's faithfulness.

Friend, God truly does supply all of your needs. Trust Him today with every area of your life. He is faithful!

Your unfailing love, O LORD, is as vast as the heavens; your faithfulness reaches beyond the clouds (Psalm 36:5).

This I Believe
I will trust God with my desires and
listen for the Holy Spirit's leading.

Trials

In the midst of trials, I suspect we all have asked God to remove the heavy weight from our shoulders. It's like the story of an old grandfather clock. It had spent years keeping the correct time. That is, until the owner, realizing how faithful the timepiece had been, showed pity.

He said, "Such an old clock; it's a shame it's carried those heavy weights year after year." So he took off the weights. And the clock stopped!

So often we long for an uncomplicated life of greater ease. But God knows exactly how much weight we can bear. Jesus never told us to lay down our crosses; He said to pick them up, to let Him place His yoke upon us.

Dear one, let Jesus give you the necessary strength to make life's journey profitable.

> *[Jesus said,] "If any of you wants to be my follower,
> you must turn from your selfish ways, take up
> your cross daily, and follow me"* (Luke 9:23).

This I Believe
In good times and bad,
God gives me strength and blessings.

Irony and Possibilities

The dictionary says "irony" is an expression marked by deliberate contrast. For example, take the fire in the Denver area where a huge warehouse was destroyed. It was ironic. Why? Because the building was filled with water—water that couldn't be used because it was frozen. That's right. The structure contained blocks of ice—thousands of gallons of potential fire extinguishing liquid, but in the wrong form so none of it was useful to the firefighters.

And what about the irony in your life? What possibilities do you have where you work, where you live, where you fellowship? Do you have assets that are frozen, that are not being used? God has called you to meet the spiritual needs of those around you. Dear one, let your heart be warmed and set ablaze with God's power. Take the good news to those without Christ.

> *If you are wise and understand God's ways, prove it
> by living an honorable life, doing good works with
> the humility that comes from wisdom* (James 3:13).

This I Believe
I want the Holy Spirit to fill
my heart with His fire.

Jesus, I Love You

Tammy and her husband, Trent, went to Jamaica for a vacation. Trent was an expert diver. On their last day, he suited up to explore the blue lagoon. Tammy took a couple of pictures and watched him swim away. She never saw him alive again. A diving team was called in to look for him.

Tammy cried out to God in her time of agony. She sang praise songs, prayed, and trusted God. The next day divers found Trent's body. Each day Tammy still deals with many emotions. But through her tears she can say, "Jesus, I love You."

Friend, Psalm 46:1 says, "God is our refuge and strength, always ready to help in times of trouble." When it seems like your world is crumbling, look to God. He will carry you through any situation.

> *[The LORD] renews my strength. He guides me along right paths, bringing honor to his name. Even when I walk through the darkest valley, I will not be afraid, for you are close beside me* (Psalm 23:3-4).

This I Believe
Even when the world seems dark,
God is with me, protecting me.

Kirsten's Story

One morning after dropping off students, a school bus driver noticed a young woman lying in the street. She called an ambulance, but it was too late. She found out later from the woman's sister that she had died from a seizure.

When Pam, Kirsten's sister, was sorting through her sister's belongings, she found a Bible. A verse in Isaiah was underlined and starred: "Fear not, for I am with you; be not dismayed, for I am your God. I will strengthen you, yes, I will help you, I will uphold you with my righteous right hand" (41:10 NKJV). Pam smiled as she thought of Kirsten, who was now free from pain and experiencing God face-to-face. What could be better than that?

Dear friend, whatever comes your way, turn to God and His Word for strength and courage.

I pray that from [God's] glorious, unlimited resources he will empower you with inner strength through his Spirit. Then Christ will make his home in your hearts as you trust in him. Your roots will grow down into God's love and keep you strong (Ephesians 3:16-17).

This I Believe
When I am discouraged, I need to change
my focus from me to God.

Make a Date

Amy was a third-grade teacher. One of her students was writing a letter to a pen pal and asked for help with punctuation and penmanship. At the bottom of the letter, Amy read: "I love the Lord, do you?" She questioned the student, named Stephanie, about that.

With a smile the student replied, "I've been a Christian for two weeks. I got a *Jesus* video in the mail and watched it by myself. Now my family is taking me to church!" Soon Stephanie was asking *all* of her classmates if they knew Jesus.

Dear friend, Jesus said, "Let the children come to me." Take the opportunity to teach a child about Jesus. Today's children will be the ones who pass Christ's message on to the next generation. So make a date with a little one today.

Jesus said, "Let the children come to me. Don't stop them! For the Kingdom of Heaven belongs to those who are like these children." And he placed his hands on their heads and blessed them before he left (Matthew 19:14-15).

This I Believe
My investment in the life of a child
will bear eternal rewards.

Perpetua

A woman named Perpetua was 22 years of age when she became a Christian in AD 202. The emperor of Rome declared she must be punished for that decision. In spite of pleading from family and friends, Perpetua was brutally put to death for her faith.

Christian women living in the United States generally don't worry about being put to death. But we do worry about what other people think and about opening ourselves up to ridicule. That kind of thinking can be lethal to our faith, and we need to know how to combat it.

Wherever God puts you, whether on the school board, at a workplace, or in your community, boldly stand for the principles He has outlined in the Bible. You can expect persecution, but God is faithful. He will stand by you.

> *[Jesus said,] "I have told you all this so that you may have peace in me. Here on earth you will have many trials and sorrows. But take heart, because I have overcome the world"* (John 16:33).

This I Believe
Nothing can keep me from sharing my faith.

The Presence of Peace

Fear has a way of finding us. Darlene Rose knows that. She and her husband were young missionaries in New Guinea. World War II broke out, and they were taken prisoner. Men and women were in separate camps, and Darlene never saw her husband again.

Darlene was accused of being a spy and spent many sleepless nights on death row. She was restless until she prayed for God's help. In that moment, Darlene felt as if God's arms went around her…holding her.

Dear one, what are you afraid of right now? Some of our fears are based on reality and some are imagined. God knows about your fears. Take them to Him. He says, "I will never fail you. I will never abandon you." If you know Him, God is with you in the midst of *every* circumstance.

> Don't worry about anything; instead, pray about
> everything. Tell God what you need, and thank him
> for all he has done. Then you will experience God's
> peace, which exceeds anything we can understand.
> His peace will guard your hearts and minds as
> you live in Christ Jesus (Philippians 4:6-7).

This I Believe
When I walk in the peace of God, the events of
my life take on new perspective.

Proper Offerings

You may have heard the story of a farmer whose cow had given birth to two calves. Being a faithful person, he promised his wife he would give one to God and keep one for them. Unfortunately, a few weeks later, one of the calves became sick and died. The farmer announced sadly to his wife, "Honey, I'm sorry to say, the Lord's cow died!"

We smile at this story, but I wonder...Do we ever do that with our stewardship? How often do we give to God what is easy, not necessarily what is right. King David, the psalmist, said, "I will not present burnt offerings that have cost me nothing" (1 Chronicles 21:24).

Everything we really want costs us something, and often that means sacrifice. Our sacrifice may be time, talents, money, patience. How do you give back to God? In light of all He's done for you—providing His Son as your Savior—give Him your very best.

What mighty praise, O God, belongs to you in Zion. We will fulfill our vows to you, for you answer our prayers. All of us must come to you (Psalm 65:1-2).

This I Believe
I love Jesus. I will honor Him by
giving Him my best.

Stale Faith

Of all my favorite aromas, one of them has to be baking bread. Ah, fresh bread just out of the oven. You can't beat it! And isn't it a shame the bread can spoil just 10 days later? In many ways, our faith is like that too. Those first few days, weeks, and months are oh so delightful, and we enjoy our new relationship with Jesus Christ. But how quickly things can go bad if we leave our faith on a shelf, hidden and unattended.

It's so important we begin our days with the Bread of Life—Jesus Christ. The Bible says, "The faithful love of the LORD never ends! His mercies never cease. Great is his faithfulness; his mercies begin afresh each morning" (Lamentations 3:22-23).

I remember your genuine faith... This is why I remind you to fan into flames the spiritual gift God gave you when I laid my hands on you (2 Timothy 1:5-6).

This I Believe
It is my responsibility to keep my faith fresh and growing.

The 28-day Challenge

Marci was dissatisfied with her walk with God. Her spiritual fruit looked very raisinlike. She talked with her heavenly Father only when convenient or in church. Her Bible was rarely opened. So Marci created a 28-day spiritual plan to draw closer to God. After those four weeks, she saw God move in her life like never before.

How can you get your spiritual growth started or restarted?

- Choose an achievable goal. Wake up 15 minutes earlier to pray. Read a chapter or two of the Bible daily.

- Begin a diary to view your progress.

- Tell a friend and be accountable to her. She may wish to join you!

Friend, create your own plan, but begin today. Like Marci, you'll see God moving in your life in new and mighty ways. You'll be amazed at the fruit He produces in your life.

> *O LORD, hear me as I pray; pay attention to my groaning. Listen to my cry for help, my King and my God, for I pray to no one but you. Listen to my voice in the morning, LORD. Each morning I bring my requests to you and wait expectantly* (Psalm 5:1-3).

This I Believe

My commitment to spend time each day with God is the foundation of my life.

Show You Care

As a college student, Vanessa tried to escape life by using alcohol and partying. Heather began to pray for Vanessa and showed kindness to her. Vanessa soon noticed there was something different about Heather and her lifestyle.

When Heather invited Vanessa to a weekly Bible study on campus, she accepted. She also asked many questions about God that Heather patiently answered. As a biology major, Vanessa realized how perfectly the world was created. It wasn't long before she gave her heart and life to the Creator. Soon Vanessa's partying friends were asking about the change in her life. She was excited to tell them about Jesus Christ.

My friend, the apostle Paul always wanted his actions to communicate the love of Christ. If you are a believer, non-Christians are watching you. Let your actions draw people to your Lord and Savior.

We live in such a way that no one will stumble because of us, and no one will find fault with our ministry. In everything we do, we show that we are true ministers of God. We patiently endure troubles and hardships and calamities of every kind (2 Corinthians 6:3-4).

This I Believe
The more I understand God's love
for me, the more I can share
His love with others.

The Big "C"

Janet Thompson taught groups of women and spoke at conferences. As she did, she was haunted by the fact that one in seven women in the room would contract breast cancer. She would squeak out a little prayer: "Lord, please don't let it be me."

But then it *was* her. Cancer was confirmed. And Janet realized every time she had cried, "Don't let it be me," it was as if God answered, "Why *not* you?" She now understood He had a purpose and plan for her breast cancer. He is using her story to reach out and comfort women who are undergoing similar trials.

Dear one, God has a purpose for whatever you're experiencing. Let Him use you in someone's life. The Bible says to comfort those who need comforting.

All praise to God, the Father of our Lord Jesus Christ. God is our merciful Father and the source of all comfort. He comforts us in all our troubles so that we can comfort others. When they are troubled, we will be able to give them the same comfort God has given us (2 Corinthians 1:3-4).

This I Believe
Every difficult experience affords me an opportunity to rely on God's comfort.

Box of Books

Two loving parents were heartsick to see their son drift away from God. He ran with a bad crowd. His parents gave him a copy of *Left Behind*—the story of the return of Jesus written by Tim LaHaye and Jerry Jenkins. The parents prayed their boy would read it.

Eventually he did. And then he told his parents they wouldn't have to worry about him any longer. He returned to God and the church. He planned to buy copies of the book and give one to each of his rowdy friends. But before he could do that, he was killed in a car accident.

His parents bought *Left Behind* books in his honor and gave them to his friends who attended the funeral. Several of them asked Jesus into their lives as a result.

Our lives are a Christ like fragrance rising up to God. But this fragrance is perceived differently by those who are being saved and by those who are perishing. To those who are perishing, we are a dreadful smell of death and doom. But to those who are being saved, we are a life-giving perfume (2 Corinthians 2:15-16).

This I Believe

Jesus will return someday. I will be ready.
I won't be left behind!

Christ in College

Vicki Courtney was a junior in college. She considered herself an agnostic. She believed it was impossible to know whether or not God exists. Believing that lie made her life empty. When someone invited her to a Christian event for college students, she made excuses for not attending a few times, but finally she went. And there she heard clearly that God loved her. Vicki prayed and surrendered her heart to Jesus!

A fellow student emphasized the importance of discipleship. Vicki followed his advice by joining the church that sponsored the event. She became involved in Campus Crusade for Christ. Months later Vicki married the advice-giver.

Let's be persistent in leading others to Jesus. We can make a difference for Christ at our schools and where we work.

You died to this life, and your real life is hidden with Christ in God. And when Christ, who is your life, is revealed to the whole world, you will share in all his glory (Colossians 3:3-4).

This I Believe
I can be the friend God uses
to deliver His message of salvation.

"Christianeze"

As a young girl, Erni enjoyed attending many Vacation Bible schools. At the end of one week's session, the children were asked to raise their hands if they were "saved." Erni had never heard that term and wasn't sure what it meant so she purposefully kept her hand down.

Many years later, a loving and patient pastor's wife befriended Erni. She explained that "saved" means "to be rescued from the penalty of disobeying God." We all fall short of God's glorious ideal, she shared, but thankfully Jesus died to pay that penalty. Erni soon prayed and invited Jesus to come into her heart.

Sometimes we talk about our faith using religious terms—Christianeze. When we share our faith with others, let's remember to make it understandable to them where they are. That's what Jesus did.

> *Jesus always used stories and illustrations like these when speaking to the crowds. In fact, he never spoke to them without using such parables. This fulfilled what God had spoken through the prophet: "I will speak to you in parables. I will explain things hidden since the creation of the world"* (Matthew 13:34-35).

This I Believe
Jesus set an example for how
to share His story.

Common Goal

Three women met for prayer and Bible study. They discovered they had a common goal—they wanted to share the good news of Jesus Christ with their neighbors. They decided to go door-to-door in their neighborhoods once a week for a few hours.

The ladies were nervous. They met for prayer first and felt God giving them His courage to proceed. With Bibles under their arms or tucked into their purses, they ventured out that first morning and visited nine homes. Four of their neighbors invited Jesus into their hearts. The next week, three more gave their lives to Jesus! The three women faithfully continue to tell others about Jesus.

Dear one, God does great things through people who make themselves available to be used by Him. He will do the same through you—if you let Him.

I thank Christ Jesus our Lord, who has given me strength to do his work. He considered me trustworthy and appointed me to serve him (1 Timothy 1:12-13).

This I Believe
Availability is more important than ability.

Daughters

Ruth's family gathered at her grandmother's home for a reunion. On the last day of their time together, Ruth's daughter bumped a precious vase, and it hit the floor and shattered. Ruth was embarrassed and angry. She picked up the pieces in a hurry. Her daughter stepped back when she realized how upset her mother was.

Just then a friend called to remind Ruth that it was the first anniversary of the death of a mutual friend, who happened to be the same age as Ruth's daughter. Ruth hung up the phone and tucked it into her pocket. She then wrapped her arms around her daughter. The broken vase was no longer an issue.

My friend, never put material things ahead of those dear ones with whom you hope to share eternity. In the words of Jim Elliot, "He is no fool who gives what he cannot keep to gain what he cannot lose."

Always be humble and gentle. Be patient with each other, making allowance for each other's faults because of your love. Make every effort to keep yourselves united in the Spirit, binding yourselves together with peace (Ephesians 4:2-3).

This I Believe
Only my relationship with God is more important than my relationships with the people around me.

Don't Wait

Midge is a widow who ignored God for 67 years. Her husband had attended church, and she'd tagged along. She'd *claimed* to be a Christian, but deep in her heart she wasn't sure.

Midge's daughter tried to speak to her about Jesus, but talking about God always made Midge upset. She did many good things for people and thought that was enough. Then Midge began having chest pains. She was scared. Suddenly she was ready to listen. From the hospital, she called her daughter. They talked, and Midge learned that she needed to choose God. She invited Jesus to take over her life…and to forgive her for thinking she could earn a place in heaven. Midge began a new life with Jesus that day.

And, friend, you can too. Believe in and receive Jesus Christ. He promises you eternal life with Him in heaven.

Even when I walk through the darkest valley, I will
not be afraid, for you are close beside me. Your rod
and your staff protect and comfort me (Psalm 23:4).

This I Believe
The assurance of salvation is available
to anyone who believes.

Dormant Seed

At age 11, Kris invited Jesus into his heart while at camp. But when he returned home, that seed of faith went dormant. Ten years later, a friend invited him to camp again. Kris had been out of college just a few months and had no job. He'd sent out 50 resumes, hoping to get into the entertainment industry, but he hadn't received even *one* response.

Kris went to the camp, and there a friend led him in prayer. Kris asked God for a job. The day after he returned home, there was a job offer from Warner Brothers! The seed of faith that had been planted so many years ago finally took root. Today, Kris Young is sharing Christ through writing.

Friend, nurture your seed of faith. When your faith grows, your life will blossom.

There is no judgment against anyone who believes in [Jesus]. But anyone who does not believe in him has already been judged for not believing in God's one and only Son (John 3:18).

This I Believe

There are many people with dormant
faith seeds that need to be watered.

Finding Life's Purpose

Evelyn was frustrated and depressed. She was struggling to find purpose for her life. She knew God had *something* in store, but she wondered what it was. She asked God to reveal her life's assignment.

Soon after she prayed, Evelyn visited a friend who had cancer. They laughed and laughed together. Later, the woman's husband told Evelyn she had a gift for helping people forget about their problems. Evelyn was ecstatic. It was finally clear! *That* was her purpose. Evelyn thanked God for showing her and for the joy knowing brought her. She sat down and wrote all the ideas that came to her mind for helping the sick and elderly focus on joy and forget about their worries for a little while.

Dear friend, you have a God-given purpose too. It may not be obvious, and if you're not sure what it is, ask God to show you. He will!

You will show me the way of life, granting me the joy of your presence and the pleasures of living with you forever (Psalm 16:11).

This I Believe

The joy of the Lord is contagious.

Forgiveness Is a Choice

It was probably the hardest spiritual test Donna Eubank had ever experienced. The Bible says to forgive, but how could she forgive the hit-and-run driver who had run into her husband and son? The two had been bicycling home when they were struck. Her husband wasn't seriously injured, but their five-year-old son had been crushed under the car. Forgiveness seemed impossible.

God's Word says, "When you are praying, first forgive anyone you are holding a grudge against, so that your Father in heaven will forgive your sins, too" (Mark 11:25). Donna was eventually able to forgive that driver—but only through the grace of God. Grace is "God's ability in us, as Christians, to do what we're unable to do in and of ourselves."

Forgiveness is a choice, not a feeling. Not forgiving fuels anger and bitterness. Forgiving frees you and the offender. Do you need to forgive someone?

Make allowance for each other's faults, and forgive anyone who offends you. Remember, the Lord forgave you, so you must forgive others (Colossians 3:13).

This I Believe
Forgiveness opens my heart to
receive God's blessing.

God Fills Empty Hearts

Carol was lonely…even though she was surrounded by crowds of people. And her depression was growing. One day she walked into a diner and slumped into a booth. She overheard two women behind her talking about God. When they prayed, God seemed like He was their best friend. Their God sounded so approachable that it touched her heart. She wanted to know more!

When the women finished praying, Carol spoke up. The women invited her to sit with them. They told her about Jesus' love, and Carol asked Him into her heart that day. The lonely void in her life was forever gone.

Dear friend, let God fill the emptiness in your life. Go to Him in prayer and invite Him into your heart. He's all you'll ever need.

You, dear friends, must build each other up in your most holy faith, pray in the power of the Holy Spirit, and await the mercy of our Lord Jesus Christ, who will bring you eternal life. In this way, you will keep yourselves safe in God's love (Jude 20-21).

This I Believe

God can use my conversations
to reach someone's heart.

God Still Does Miracles

It's true! God still does miracles. And when someone invites Jesus into his or her life, God miraculously changes that person. Sometimes it's not very noticeable, but in this case it was.

Christian hip-hop artist "T-Bone" was in concert. In the middle of the music, he stopped and began preaching about God's love. He didn't know it, but several gang members were in the audience. They were there to kill someone.

After they heard God's Word and T-Bone's story, they gave their hearts to Jesus! The gang leader walked forward and put his gun down where T-Bone had given an altar call. His gang followed, placing their guns and gang-colored rags there as well. Then they went to the man they had planned to murder and hugged him. They asked for forgiveness.

Friend, let God do a miracle in your life.

Now we can rejoice in our wonderful new relationship with God because our Lord Jesus Christ has made us friends of God (Romans 5:11).

This I Believe
Salvation is the greatest miracle of all.

God's Prompting

Author Fran Sandin felt God prompting her to give the woman next to her one of her books. They were waiting for a delayed flight, and the book touched off a conversation between the two strangers. Peggy revealed that her best friend's husband had taken his life the night before, and she was devastated.

The book Fran gave her contained stories of lives affected by God. God used the message of His love and faithfulness in Peggy's life. In turn, Peggy shared the book with a group of women searching for a better relationship with God.

Since that initial contact, Fran learned Peggy and her friend attended a grief recovery seminar. They began a Bible study at a local church. Peggy and her husband have both changed through their newfound relationship with Christ.

Friend, be sensitive to God's promptings.

*Lead me by your truth and teach me, for
you are the God who saves me. All day long
I put my hope in you* (Psalm 25:5).

This I Believe
God wants to use me to reach others!

With New Hope

Wanda was a high school dropout with a young son to support. At her work, she was required to wear a skimpy uniform. Before long, the lusty stares from men made her feel dirty, but she needed the job.

After work one night, Wanda went to a grocery store. She stopped by the beer section to pick up a six-pack when she saw a small leaflet on the shelf. The headline read: "Where will you spend eternity?" The question took her breath away. She took the booklet and left the beer. She read the gospel message in the booklet and learned that with Jesus she could have a new future. So she prayed and invited Him to help change her life. With new hope in her heart, she began looking for a different job the next day.

Dear friend, God's Word has the power to change your life too!

It is the same with my word. I send it out, and it always produces fruit. It will accomplish all I want it to, and it will prosper everywhere I send it (Isaiah 55:11).

This I Believe
God's Word is powerful in any form.

Only a Prayer Away

Judy's teenage life took a horrible turn. One day her boss raped her and then convinced her it was her fault. She kept the tormenting secret to herself. She longed to know real love and to feel safe from pain.

Several years later, she married a man who tenderly loved and sheltered her. Then he died in a terrible car accident. Judy couldn't bear to face life alone. She wanted to die. In fact, she entered a church to say goodbye to the world. As she prayed, she felt God's love wash over her. She wept and invited Jesus to take control of her life.

Today Judy is learning to build her life on Jesus. With His help, she *will* make it!

Dear one, you can rely on God to pull you through life's difficulties. He's only a prayer away.

Why am I discouraged? Why is my heart so sad?
I will put my hope in God! I will praise him
again—my Savior and my God! (Psalm 43:5).

This I Believe
God can rescue and restore even the
most despondent person.

Lifestyle of Worship

Krysta was tired of church. Three times a week was too much. Hearing about God on Sundays was adequate. Then a life-threatening illness forced her to spend time at home in bed, and she was in and out of the hospital. The God Krysta met quietly while reading the Bible was different than what she had experienced before. She learned to enjoy spending time with Him. Worship took on new meaning because she knew God loved her and she loved Him back. When she recovered, she continued worshiping every day.

My friend, worship is not just the time you have in church on a particular day of the week at a particular time. Worship is what you do in your everyday life—at your job, with your family and friends, and when no one is looking. A relationship with God is a *lifestyle*, not a part-time job.

Honor the LORD for the glory of his name. Worship the
LORD in the splendor of his holiness (Psalm 29:2).

This I Believe
Every moment of my life can be an
expression of worship.

Flying with Jesus

Darla was afraid to fly. She had to be medicated whenever she stepped on a plane. That is, until she was hired as a flight attendant for a major airline. Despite her apprehension, she knew God wanted her there. However, her fears were magnified after the September 11, 2001, tragedy. A week and a half after that terrorist strike, Darla regained enough composure to fly again.

Before the plane lifted off, she prayed and her fears subsided. Then she and another Christian flight attendant prayed together. Soon three more flight attendants joined them. God's peace filled the plane. Darla had many opportunities to talk about God on that flight. She continues to fly with Jesus every day.

Dear friend, bring your fears to God today. He'll give you peace in the midst of any storm.

Don't be afraid, for I am with you. Don't be discouraged, for I am your God. I will strengthen you and help you. I will hold you up with my victorious right hand (Isaiah 41:10).

This I Believe
God cares about my fears and will help me.

Sharing Jesus

Tina's parents separated and, as a result, her life was in upheaval. She was bounced from one household to another. Her parents continued to squabble about her life. Tina's mother was demanding and critical; her father was more understanding and supportive. Tina felt like a soccer ball kicked from one goal to another.

One day her father suggested she go on a mission trip that was sponsored by his church. Tina was reluctant, but to win his approval, she went. On the trip, Tina learned about God's unconditional love. She invited Jesus into her heart, and she shared her experience as part of the mission. How wonderful to find Jesus and then immediately tell others about Him!

If Jesus is in your life, are you sharing Him with others?

"Everyone who calls on the name of the Lord will be saved." But how can they call on him to save them unless they believe in him? And how can they believe in him if they have never heard about him? And how can they hear about him unless someone tells them? And how will anyone go and tell them without being sent? That is why the Scriptures say, "How beautiful are the feet of messengers who bring good news!" (Romans 10:13-15)

This I Believe
I consider it a joy and privilege to
share about Jesus.

Motorcycle Rally

Glenda's parents were alcoholics and abusive, so she ran away at age 15. She lived on the streets, getting by however she could. A handsome man "befriended" her, but he had an agenda. Instead of helping her, he got her hooked on drugs and forced her into prostitution. Glenda spent many years in that tragic lifestyle.

One day a local church hosted a motorcycle rally. Glenda loved motorcycles and decided to go. Afterward, the pastor invited everyone for refreshments. While everyone was visiting, he told them how much Jesus loved them. Glenda learned that God's gift of love is free. That day she invited Jesus into her heart. And God used that church to help her discover a brand-new lifestyle.

"Sirs, what must I do to be saved?"

They replied, "Believe in the Lord Jesus and you will be saved, along with everyone in your household." And they shared the word of the Lord with him and with all who lived in his household... Then he and everyone in his household were immediately baptized...[They] rejoiced because they all believed in God (Acts 16:30-34).

This I Believe

Through my church I can be instrumental
in helping people find Jesus.

Not Good Enough

Barbara Cameron thought she was doing well. She'd reared four happy children, two of whom became successful actors. She helped dying children and their families. She took in foster children. Yet she felt like something was missing.

Her son Kirk talked to her about God. Barbara felt she was basically a good person, but the truth in the Bible revealed the glaring error. It says that everyone falls short of God's perfect standard. Barbara realized she was like all of us—"deceitfully wicked." She sobbed over her guilt and prayed for Jesus to come into her life. She now says, "I desire to live my life according to God's standards of righteousness, not by man's standards of happiness."

Friend, Jesus is the only One who can make you right with God.

For everyone has sinned; we all fall short of God's glorious standard (Romans 3:23).

This I Believe
I want to share how much Jesus loves me so people will want what I have.

Not Me!

Merry couldn't believe she was guilty of taking someone's life. How could she have killed her unborn child? She felt lost even though she was sitting in church. She reflected on what she'd done, realizing she was disappointed and depressed.

Then she heard the sweet melody and words of "Amazing Grace," each stanza gently touching her heart. She prayed, "God, I've totally messed up my life. If You can take over and do something with it, I give it to You." It was a simple prayer of surrender.

Her life changed. Thirty-two years later, Merry still sees Christ working in her life. She tells others how God led her out of despair and gave her new hope.

My friend, do you need to turn any guilt over to God? He offers true forgiveness and a fresh start.

Come quickly, LORD, and answer me, for my depression deepens. Don't turn away from me, or I will die. Let me hear of your unfailing love each morning, for I am trusting you. Show me where to walk, for I give myself to you (Psalm 143:7-8).

This I Believe
I will be brave today and share God's love.

Performing for God

Beth was reared in a church-attending family, went to a church-sponsored school, memorized the names of the books of the Bible, and received an "A" in religion class. But she was just performing for God.

Then a volleyball injury and her grandfather's death knocked her "perfect" world apart, and Beth fell into despair. While in college, a friend shared Campus Crusade for Christ's *Four Spiritual Laws* booklet with her. For the first time, Beth understood that Jesus was interested in a *personal relationship* with her, not just her religious performance. She decided to follow Him! And now author Beth Lueders continues to share her faith through her writing.

God doesn't want you to perform for Him. He wants a personal relationship with you.

God saved you by his grace when you believed. And you can't take credit for this; it is a gift from God. Salvation is not a reward for the good things we have done, so none of us can boast about it (Ephesians 2:8-9).

This I Believe

I want to help people understand
they can't earn God's love.
God's love is a free gift!

Wanting More

When Shirley was a child she attended church. But as she grew up, she struggled with why Christ had to suffer and die. When she watched televised crusades, she wondered if she was missing something. Could God really be personally interested in her? She longed for Him to be part of her everyday life. She wanted more than just putting in a quick prayer before meals or at bedtime. She yearned for Him to be the center of her marriage and decision making.

Then one evening Shirley prayed and told God she was through debating. She invited Jesus to come into her heart. She finally understood that because God is holy and perfect, she could never stand before Him on her own merit.

And that's why God sent Jesus to die for us. Jesus paid the penalty for our sins. And friend, God died for you too. He wants to know you personally.

Even before he made the world, God loved us and chose us in Christ to be holy and without fault in his eyes (Ephesians 1:4).

This I Believe
I'm so glad God loves me!

Relentless Pursuit

God continually pursues His children. And many times, He uses someone in our lives to lead us to Him. That's what He did in Jackie's life. A group of friends at Jackie's high school prayed she would come to a youth Bible study. Because her friends kept inviting her, Jackie finally agreed to attend. At the meeting, one of the teenagers shared the gospel. Jackie prayed and invited Jesus into her heart!

No one in the Bible study knew the horrible home life Jackie faced every day, but God did. And He used that precious group of young people to lead their friend to Him. Jackie was spared not only from hell, but also from a family pattern of suicide, drugs, and alcohol.

Friend, there may be a "Jackie" that God has placed in your life. Pursue her!

I will praise the LORD at all times. I will constantly speak his praises. I will boast only in the LORD; let all who are helpless take heart. Come, let us tell of the LORD's greatness; let us exalt his name together (Psalm 34:1-3).

This I Believe
I will look for someone I can
share Jesus with today.

Treasuring Emily

Emily was a fragile baby. At just two days old, she suffered a severe brain hemorrhage. Yet she was stronger than she looked, so she survived. Emily was profoundly impaired mentally, but that didn't stop her family from loving her.

The little girl spread sunshine everywhere she went. Not through her words though. She couldn't talk. It wasn't through her actions either. She could barely move. Despite her overwhelming disabilities, her soul and sweet spirit showed the love and peace of God to everyone around her.

Emily's family learned to value her as a treasure. She wasn't a burden. They believed God sent Emily to them to teach them incredible lessons about Him.

Friend, what heavy burden are you carrying? Ask God to show you how to treasure the difficulties He's allowed into your life.

[God says,] "Call on me when you are in trouble, and I will rescue you, and you will give me glory" (Psalm 50:15).

This I Believe
God will give me strength for every challenge I face.

Bruised Reeds

I n 1981, Barbara Sullivan was invited to a state drug treatment facility to lead a Bible study for the women residents. Several ladies from her church nervously joined her. These were middle-class suburban homemakers, none of whom had a drug background or had racial similarities with the residents. They decided they would just share how Jesus had changed their lives.

The facility's residents had the freedom to leave the Bible study anytime, but they stayed and listened. God broke down barriers, and His love poured out. Walls of prejudice came down, and new friendships were forged. A number of the women invited Jesus into their lives.

God wants to use you to reach those you might not expect. He will give you the courage and ability. He can and will do a mighty work through you.

> *He will not crush the weakest reed or put out a*
> *flickering candle. Finally he will cause justice*
> *to be victorious. And his name will be the hope*
> *of all the world* (Matthew 12:20-21).

This I Believe
God gives me so much love
that I want to—I need to—share it!

Thanks from the Heart

Thank you. These two words are one of the first things we teach our children to say because we want them to be aware of how they've been blessed. We love to hear children spontaneously thank someone. It's refreshing to be around people who demonstrate an attitude of gratefulness.

The opposite is true, as well, It's unpleasant to be around people who are ungrateful. According to Luke 17, Jesus was on His way to Galilee. He passed through a village where ten men afflicted with leprosy cried out for Him to have pity on them and heal them. Jesus did! The men were completely renewed. But only one man thanked Jesus.

Do you find that as strange as I did at first? Then I realized I often make the same mistake. I don't always go running back to glorify the Lord and give Him thanks for His many blessings.

We thank you, O God! We give thanks because you are near. People everywhere tell of your wonderful deeds (Psalm 75:1).

This I Believe
I will give glory and thanks to God for *all* that He does and for all that He is.

To Believe

In the 1800s a missionary in the southwestern Pacific islands began to translate the Scripture into a native tongue. Before long he ran into a major hurdle. The people had no word equivalent to "believe." For weeks the translator struggled to find a word to help the people know what it means to believe.

One day, a worker came into the missionary's office, worn out from a hard day. He collapsed into a nearby chair. As he breathed a contented sigh of relief, he told the missionary it felt good to lean his whole weight on the chair.

That was it! "Lean your whole weight on." He'd finally found the right words to explain the concept "to believe."

Believing in God has nothing to do with the strength or size of our belief, but it has everything to do with the One in whom we believe.

Trust in the LORD with all your heart; do not depend on your own understanding (Proverbs 3:5).

This I Believe

I can lean the whole weight of my world on Jesus—
my cares, my concerns, my heartaches.

Help!

A woman was riding her bike. A river sparkled beside her, and the sun was shining brightly. Her serenity was interrupted by screams: "Help! You've got to help me!" She searched the river and saw a woman in trouble. Without hesitation, she jumped off her bike and slid down the embankment. She ran into the water and waded out to help the drowning woman. But the current was stronger than she anticipated, and suddenly they were both moving rapidly downstream. She realized they were in trouble and also began calling for help.

Three people were on a ledge watching. Two were even videotaping their plight.

"We're drowning! Help!" the women cried.

The spectators ran to the water and waded in. Forming a human chain, they caught and pulled the women to safety.

Friend, our nation is sinking into moral decay. Reach out with the lifesaving love of Jesus.

What joy for the nation whose God is the LORD, whose people he has chosen as his inheritance (Psalm 33:12).

This I Believe

Working together, we can make a difference,
helping to shape our nation for future generations
to enjoy and give glory to God.

In His Presence

Are you too busy with family, work, church, and social activities? Does this busyness make you long for a moment to catch your breath? Perhaps your life is like Vicky's. She was in graduate school finishing a master's degree in counseling. She was also working and seeing clients. Suddenly her busy life came to a screeching halt.

Doctors discovered Vicky had a rare blood disorder. She spent 13 days in the hospital and had several plasma transfusions. During this period of uncertainty, she leaned on God and experienced His presence and joy in new ways.

Sometimes we get so busy we forget to stop and enjoy God's presence. Unfortunately, it can take a tragedy or illness to slow us down. Only then do we reevaluate our lives and reconnect with God more often.

My dear one, follow Jesus' example and connect with God daily.

Before daybreak the next morning, Jesus got up and went out to an isolated place to pray (Mark 1:35).

This I Believe
I will find true rest in Jesus' presence.

A Simple Heart

When Bill and I signed a contract to become slaves of Jesus Christ, we committed to not accumulate possessions. The contract was not an attempt to simplify our lives, but a covenant with God to prioritize serving Him. Simplicity is not the absence of "things" or activities. A simple heart can embrace activities with a deliberate attitude of accomplishment, knowing that his or her priorities have been guided by the Holy Spirit.

Simplicity is also not a matter of style, but rather an *attitude of the heart*. Hearts surrendered to Christ have a priority that impacts every thought and activity: serving Jesus. Compassion flows from our hearts and prompts us to provide for the needs of others. Healing words are spoken more deliberately, and anger is replaced by patience and forgiveness.

Those who love their life in this world will lose it. Those who care nothing for their life in this world will keep it for eternity (John 12:25).

This I Believe
Dying to self and making Christ my priority
eternally enriches my life.

A Willing Heart

"God is more interested in availability than ability." Bill said that so often it became our philosophy. Being available to God comes naturally to those who choose Christ's path. I have seen young and old believers timidly step out in faith to serve and grow spiritually stronger. Women around the world are making a positive impact on people and cultures for Jesus because they choose to be available.

"Being available" doesn't have to mean leaving our husbands and homes to serve in remote locales. Neither is it a passive attitude where we wait for service opportunities to drop into our laps. We need to *ask God for guidance* and then *seek opportunities* to share our faith and demonstrate a biblical worldview.

As we actively pursue a deeper relationship with God, He will send opportunities beyond our wildest imaginations—but we must accept them.

I was chosen to explain to everyone this mysterious plan that God, the Creator of all things, had kept secret from the beginning (Ephesians 3:9).

This I Believe

When my heart is directed by the Holy Spirit and
I embrace the challenge at hand,
God will help me accomplish great things for Him.

A Gift Every Day

A gift is at your door every morning! The new day can be treasured and used to bring glory and honor to the giver of the gift—the Lord God. Each day brings challenges and trials that can overwhelm us and keep us from seeing the possibilities available. And many of us tend to carry the burdens of yesterday into our present day.

My friend, Jesus came to give us a life free of the burdens of sin and filled with hope. Enjoying the freshness of each day is up to you. And when you don't understand what God is doing, remind yourself of God's great grace and receive His gift of forgiveness. A whispered prayer is the guarantee of a fresh start.

No, dear brothers and sisters, I have not achieved it, but I focus on this one thing: Forgetting the past and looking forward to what lies ahead, I press on to reach the end of the race and receive the heavenly prize for which God, through Christ Jesus, is calling us (Philippians 3:13-14).

This I Believe
With prayer, the beauty of life comes
into clear view.

A Good Distraction

Many years ago I was on a flight just days after a horrible plane crash in the Everglades that killed hundreds of passengers. As the flight attendants served a snack, a little eight-year-old girl preceded them down the aisle. She stopped to ask each passenger, "Would you like some chips?" The attendant explained that "when she got on board in Atlanta, she was terrified. She had never flown, and she kept talking about what had happened in the Everglades. She asked if we'd heard about the crash. We decided to get her involved in helping us to alleviate her fear. And now she's as happy as can be!" Being a little hostess was the best thing for the little girl.

That's a wonderful illustration of Acts 20:35: "It is more blessed to give than to receive." The person who gives focuses outside herself. And she's usually happier than people who don't give.

Learn to do good. Seek justice. Help the oppressed. Defend the cause of orphans. Fight for the rights of widows (Isaiah 1:17).

This I Believe

God is big enough and caring enough to meet my needs, so I can help meet the needs of others.

A Woman's Heart

Countless volumes have been written to help men and women understand the differences between them. Some differences are so obvious we smile, while some are much subtler. Our attitudes and actions reflect our basic beliefs about the roles and responsibilities God outlines in His Word.

We need to understand two important concepts from Colossians 3: "voluntary submission" and "sacrificial love." What a difference these can make in our attitudes toward our spouses. If we truly honor each other as individuals and demonstrate respect, most challenges in our marriage relationships can be toned down or eliminated. When we accept the guidelines in God's Word as a pattern for our lives, we will experience fulfillment and satisfaction. The tendency to compete with our husbands will be replaced with a desire to complement them.

Jesus saw people equally, regardless of gender.

Wives, submit to your husbands, as is fitting for those who belong to the Lord. Husbands, love your wives and never treat them harshly (Colossians 3:18-19).

This I Believe

God's forgiveness touches every heart. This helps me function in harmony with others.

Faith Is Not a Feeling

Ney Bailey, barely three feet tall and scared to death, stood on the edge of the pool. Her father was in the water, coaxing her to jump in.

"Jump in, Ney! I'll catch you!"

Finally Ney jumped. Her head went under, and she came up sputtering and thrashing.

Her father had moved back in the water, hoping she would swim to him.

Ney cried, "Daddy, you moved! You said you'd catch me!"

Her father laughed and said, "Ney, you know I wouldn't let anything happen to you."

Ney's trust was broken. Over the years this evolved into anger and bitterness. A deep rift grew between father and daughter.

While at college, Ney gave her life to Christ. She learned that faith *is not* a feeling. Faith means *believing God* and choosing to be obedient, regardless of emotions. Based on God's Word, Ney chose to love her father regardless of his actions. She asked him to forgive her bitterness. He did— and now their relationship is strong.

> *If you forgive those who sin against you, your*
> *heavenly Father will forgive you* (Matthew 6:14).

This I Believe
Giving my hard feelings to God removes
turmoil and anger from my life.

Genuine Encouragement

Jealousy, nitpicking, selfish agendas—yes, even Christians deal with these attitudes and feelings. To be effective in God's work, we need to put others before ourselves. Here are three C's of encouragement to consider:

compliment, confidence, compassion

To *compliment* a friend means to tell her what you appreciate about her. Not idle flattery or back-patting, this is true admiration founded on solid evidence.

To express *confidence* is to show you believe in her. You encourage her to excel. If she has made a mistake, your confidence in her may help her begin again.

To show *compassion* is letting her know you support her. Instead of offering advice, you listen to her share her pain, reveal your own failures, and let her know you identify with her, that she is not alone.

Let's use the three "C's" to reach out to people in God's name.

Let everything you say be good and helpful, so that your words will be an encouragement (Ephesians 4:29).

This I Believe
I can put people's needs before my own.

Little Children

When I see families, I'm reminded of how hard it is to be parents and how important it is to nurture children physically and emotionally. Jesus cared deeply about children and gave them His undivided attention.

The responsibilities of motherhood can seem relentless and frustrating. Yet after God and your husband, there is no greater priority than your children. If you feel overwhelmed, anxious, or even angry by that burden, please seek help. Those emotions are normal, and people will help you know what to do. Talk to a friend, a pastor, or someone else you trust.

Make sure you seize every opportunity to demonstrate kindness to your kids. There are thousands of ways to make them feel special. You can walk with them, buy something they are selling for school, read something they have written, and listen to them read aloud.

> *Jesus said, "Let the children come to me. Don't stop them! For the Kingdom of Heaven belongs to those who are like these children." And he placed his hands on their heads and blessed them* (Matthew 19:14-15).

This I Believe
My children need my encouragement.

Curiosity or Belief?

Lisa attended a Bible study every week. She made it clear that her attendance was because of curiosity, not belief. One day the leader approached Lisa and asked, "What do you think about what you've been learning from the Bible?"

Lisa quickly replied, "Do you want to be my friend or just convert me?"

Gently the leader responded, "More than anything else in life, I want you to know Jesus. But if you never believe, Lisa, I'll still love you."

Every week Lisa shared with her husband what she was discovering in the Bible. He was curious too. Soon he began meeting regularly with a Christian man who answered his questions and shared Jesus.

One morning, Lisa called her Bible-study leader. She shared that her husband had tossed and turned all night. Then he went downstairs, knelt, and chose to trust Jesus Christ!

It is the same with my word. I send it out, and it always produces fruit. It will accomplish all I want it to, and it will prosper everywhere I send it (Isaiah 55:11).

This I Believe
If I share Jesus and the Scriptures,
God will do the rest.

Beyond Maintenance

Most of the hours in our day are spent on maintenance—doing what must be done again the next day. If we aren't careful, we can spend the majority of time getting by and never pressing forward to expand our minds and broaden our scope of influence.

Women have a wonderful ability to balance many tasks and to patiently work toward the completion of long-term goals. But developing goals without a strategy for achieving them often brings frustration and defeat. I encourage you to prayerfully ask God to guide you as you develop a strategy for your life. Spend time in His Word and, after prayerful consideration, write out some goals and ideas for achieving them. You can then easily determine how many activities in your day support or detract from your life strategy and prioritize as needed.

Make sure your life strategy is flexible enough to allow for any God-directed detours!

Work willingly at whatever you do, as though you were working for the Lord rather than for people (Colossians 3:23).

This I Believe
My life strategy is based on God's guidance.
I want to bring Him glory and honor.

Intimacy with God

An actor was asked by a pastor to recite the Twenty-third Psalm. The actor agreed if the pastor would recite it also. With great resonance and eloquence, the actor said, "The Lord is my shepherd, I shall not want..." When he finished, the audience gave him a standing ovation.

The pastor had walked closely with God for years. As he recited the familiar psalm, it was apparent he believed every word. When he was done the audience was silent. Tears filled their eyes.

The actor said, "I reached your ears, but this man of God reached your hearts."

Friend, God loves you. But until you respond to Him through Jesus, you can't experience the ultimate intimacy—a personal relationship with Him.

> *[Jesus said,] "I am praying not only for these disciples but also for all who will ever believe in me through their message. I pray that they will all be one, just as you and I are one—as you are in me, Father, and I am in you. And may they be in us so that the world will believe you sent me"* (John 17:20-21).

This I Believe

God's Word gives me insights into His character.
His presence gives me peace.

Our Walk

Achievement and success are applauded. We even use the power of affirmation with our children. With cheers of joy and clapping hands, parents coax their babies to take those first brave steps. As the toddler wobbles into open arms, their smiles affirm the great accomplishment. Their encouragement helps the baby keep trying until he or she successfully walks without assistance.

In our walk with Christ, we are not called to success. Instead, we are called to be faithful. Even if our spiritual steps are unsteady at times, we must press on. Developing a life of faith requires careful attention to our choices. In many cases, seemingly insignificant options may be pivotal to being faithful to God.

Every time you take a negative thought captive or share your faith with a friend, are taking steps of faith and growing in Christ. Your heavenly Father is pleased with you!

You know that when your faith is tested, your endurance has a chance to grow. So let it grow, for when your endurance is fully developed, you will be perfect and complete, needing nothing (James 1:3-4).

This I Believe
Each new step in Christ is an achievement...
and heaven cheers.

275

Beginning Your Journey of Joy

These four principles are essential in beginning a journey of joy.

One—

God loves you and created you to know Him personally.

God's Love

"God so loved the world that He gave His one and only Son, that whoever believes in Him shall not perish but have eternal life" (John 3:16).

God's Plan

"Now this is eternal life: that they may know you, the only true God, and Jesus Christ, whom you have sent" (John 17:3).

What prevents us from knowing God personally?

Two—

People are sinful and separated from God, so we cannot know Him personally or experience His love.

People Are Sinful

"All have sinned and fall short of the glory of God" (Romans 3:23).

People were created to have fellowship with God; but, because of our own stubborn self-will, we chose to go our own independent way and fellowship with God was broken. This self-will, characterized by an attitude of active rebellion or passive indifference, is an evidence of what the Bible calls sin.

People Are Separated

"The wages of sin is death" [spiritual separation from God] (Romans 6:23).

This diagram illustrates that God is holy and people are sinful. A great gulf separates the two. The arrows illustrate that people are continually trying to reach God and establish a personal relationship with Him through our own efforts, such as a good life, philosophy, or religion—but we inevitably fail.

The third principle explains the only way to bridge this gulf...

Three—

Jesus Christ is God's only provision for our sin.
Through Him alone we can know God personally
and experience His love.

He Died in Our Place

"God demonstrates His own love toward us, in that while we were yet sinners, Christ died for us" (Romans 5:8).

He Rose from the Dead

"Christ died for our sins…He was buried…He was raised on the third day according to the Scriptures…He appeared to Peter, then to the twelve. After that He appeared to more than five hundred…" (1 Corinthians 15:3-6).

He Is the Only Way to God

"Jesus said to him, 'I am the way, and the truth, and the life; no one comes to the Father but through Me'" (John 14:6).

This diagram illustrates that God has bridged the gulf that separates us from Him by sending His Son, Jesus Christ, to die on the cross in our place to pay the penalty for our sins.

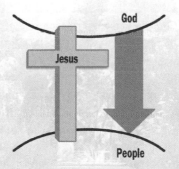

It is not enough just to know these three truths…

Four—

*We must individually receive Jesus Christ as
Savior and Lord; then we can know God
personally and experience His love.*

We Must Receive Christ

"As many as received Him, to them He gave the right to become
children of God, even to those who believe in His name" (John
1:12).

We Receive Christ Through Faith

"By grace you have been saved through faith; and that not of
yourselves, it is the gift of God; not as a result of works that no
one should boast" (Ephesians 2:8-9).

When We Receive Christ, We Experience a New Birth

(Read John 3:1-8.)

We Receive Christ by Personal Invitation

[Christ speaking] "Behold, I stand at the door and knock; if anyone hears My voice and opens the door, I will come in to him"
(Revelation 3:20).

Receiving Christ involves turning to God from self (repentance)
and trusting Christ to come into our lives to forgive us of our
sins and to make us what He wants us to be. Just to agree intel-
lectually that Jesus Christ is the Son of God and that He died
on the cross for our sins is not enough. Nor is it enough to have
an emotional experience. We receive Jesus Christ by faith, as an
act of our will.

These two circles represent two kinds of lives:

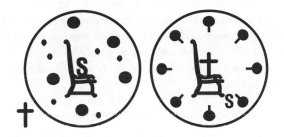

Which circle best represents your life?

Which circle would you like to have represent your life?

The following explains how you can receive Christ.

You Can Receive Christ Right Now by Faith Through Prayer

(Prayer is talking with God)

God knows your heart and is not so concerned with your words as He is with the attitude of your heart. The following is a suggested prayer:

> *Lord Jesus, I want to know You personally. Thank You for dying on the cross for my sins. I open the door of my life and receive You as my Savior and Lord. Thank You for forgiving my sins and giving me eternal life. Take control of the throne of my life. Make me the kind of person You want me to be.*

Does this prayer express the desire of your heart?

If it does, I invite you to pray this prayer right now, and Christ will come into your life, as He promised.

How to Know That Christ Is in Your Life

Did you receive Christ into your life? According to His promise in Revelation 3:20, where is Christ right now in relation to you? Christ said that He would come into your life. Would He mislead you? On what authority do you know that God has answered your prayer? (The trustworthiness of God Himself and His Word.)

The Bible Promises Eternal Life to All Who Receive Christ

"The witness is this, that God has given us eternal life, and this life is in His Son. He who has the Son has the life; he who does not have the Son of God does not have the life. These things I have written to you who believe in the name of the Son of God, in order that you may know that you have eternal life" (1 John 5:11-13).

Thank God often that Christ is in your life and that He will never leave you (Hebrews 13:5). You can know on the basis of His promise that Christ lives in you and that you have eternal life from the very moment you invite Him in. He will not deceive you.

An important reminder...

Feelings Can Be Unreliable

You might have expectations about how you should feel after placing your trust in Christ. While feelings are important, they are unreliable indicators of your sincerity or the trustworthiness of God's promise. Our feelings change easily, but God's Word and His character remain constant. This illustration shows the relationship among *fact* (God and His Word), *faith* (our trust in God and His Word), and our *feelings*.

Fact: The chair is strong enough to support you.

Faith: You believe this chair will support you, so you sit in it.

Feeling: You may or may not feel comfortable in this chair, but it continues to support you.

The promise of God's Word, the Bible—not our feelings—is our authority. The Christian lives by faith (trust) in the trustworthiness of God Himself and His Word.

Now That You Have Entered into a Personal Relationship with Christ

The moment you received Christ by faith, as an act of your will, many things happened, including the following:

- Christ came into your life (Revelation 3:20; Colossians 1:27).
- Your sins were forgiven (Colossians 1:14).
- You became a child of God (John 1:12).
- You received eternal life (John 5:24).

- You began the great adventure for which God created you (John 10:10; 2 Corinthians 5:17; 1 Thessalonians 5:18).

Can you think of anything more wonderful that could happen to you than entering into a personal relationship with Jesus Christ? Would you like to thank God in prayer right now for what He has done for you? By thanking God, you demonstrate your faith.

To enjoy your new relationship with God...

Suggestions for Christian Growth

Spiritual growth results from trusting Jesus Christ. "The righteous man shall live by faith" (Galatians 3:11). A life of faith will enable you to trust God increasingly with every detail of your life, and to practice the following:

G *Go* to God in prayer daily (John 15:7).

R *Read* God's Word daily (Acts 17:11); begin with the Gospel of John.

O *Obey* God moment by moment (John 14:21).

W *Witness* for Christ by your life and words (Matthew 4:19; John 15:8).

T *Trust* God for every detail of your life (1 Peter 5:7).

H *Holy Spirit*—allow Him to control and empower your daily life and witness (Galatians 5:16,17; Acts 1:8; Ephesians 5:18).

Fellowship in a Good Church

God's Word admonishes us not to forsake "the assembling of ourselves together" (Hebrews 10:25). Several logs burn brightly together, but put one aside on the cold hearth and the fire goes out. So it is with your relationship with other Christians. If you do not belong to a church, do not wait to be invited. Take the initiative; call the pastor of a nearby church where Christ is honored and His Word is preached. Start this week, and make plans to attend regularly.

If you would like more information about Jesus, the gospel, or sharing your faith, please visit

www.DiscoverGod.com

If you would like to contact Mrs. Bright, you can send an email to

Vonette.Bright@ccci.org